Your Labor of Love

A Spiritual Companion for Expectant Mothers

Agnes M. Penny

Your Labor of Love

A Spiritual Companion for Expectant Mothers

Agnes M. Penny

TAN BOOKS AND PUBLISHERS, INC.
Rockford, Illinois 61105

Cover photo: Katrissa Howard, whose firstborn son was born 13 days after this photo was taken. Katrissa Schneider and Martin Howard were married at a Traditional Latin Mass at St. Mary's Oratory in Rockford, Illinois on August 24, 2002.

Printed and bound in the United States of America.

TAN BOOKS AND PUBLISHERS, INC.
P.O. Box 424
Rockford, Illinois 61105
2003

To Be a Mother

"The most Important Person on earth is a mother.
She cannot claim the honor of having built
Notre Dame Cathedral. She need not.
She has built something more magnificent
than any cathedral—a dwelling for an immortal soul,
the tiny perfection of her baby's body . . .
The angels have not been blessed
with such a grace. They cannot share in God's
creative miracle to bring new saints to Heaven.
Only a human mother can.
Mothers are closer to God the Creator
than any other creature; God joins forces
with mothers in performing this act of creation. . . .
What on God's good earth is more glorious than this:
to be a mother?"

— ☩ Joseph Cardinal Mindszenty
1892-1975

To All Brave Mothers

"We would like to pay homage to all brave mothers who dedicate themselves to their own family without reserve, who suffer in giving birth to their children and who are ready to make any effort, to face any sacrifice, in order to pass on to them the best of themselves . . . How hard they have to fight against difficulties and dangers! How frequently they are called to face genuine 'wolves' determined to snatch and scatter the flock! And these heroic mothers do not always find support in their surroundings. On the contrary, the cultural models frequently promoted and broadcast by the media do not encourage motherhood. In the name of progress and modernity, the values of fidelity, chastity, sacrifice, in which a host of Christian wives and mothers have distinguished and continue to distinguish themselves, are presented as obsolete. As a result, a woman who is determined to be consistent with her principles often feels deeply alone, alone in her love which she cannot betray, and to which she must remain faithful. Her guiding principle is Christ, who has revealed the love which the Father bestows on us. A woman who believes in Christ finds a powerful support precisely in this love that bears everything. . . ."

—Pope John Paul II
On the Beatification of
Gianna Beretta Molla

A Note to the Reader

THE following thoughts are not written in long, fluid chapters, but rather, in the format of short reflections, each of which can be easily read in a few minutes; mothers are known to be busy, and long chapters, however interesting, tend to remain unread by them. Hopefully, these short reflections will be ideal for mothers who often need just a breath of inspiration between preparing tonight's casserole and getting the children up from their naps.

Also, the reader may notice that the titles of several of these meditations reflect the less pleasant aspects of pregnancy, such as tiredness, sleeplessness, worry, etc. This is not meant to discourage the reader or to portray pregnancy as a wholly negative experience. Rather, the purpose behind these headings is to assure expectant mothers that someone else understands what they are going through and will talk to them on their level. Expectant mothers will realize at once that these reflections are not too lofty or too idealistic to be of practical use. Further, when they see these seemingly "negative" headings juxtaposed with more positive headings, such as "The Vocation of Motherhood" or "Love's Great Adventure," then they will realize, before reading any single chapter, that someone else has known the same difficulties and trials that they are enduring and has nonetheless emerged from the whole process proclaiming pregnancy to be a beautiful and sanctifying experience.

Preface

*"For which cause comfort one another; and edify one another,
as you also do."* (1 Thessalonians 5:11).

CONGRATULATIONS! You are reading these
words because you have found out that you are
a mother—that you bear a new life within you,
a unique human being who would never have existed
at all except for your openness to God's sacred and
wonderful gift of life, and who will now have the chance
to be immeasurably happy with God forever and ever
in Heaven. What a glorious vocation and privilege is
yours! What joy can be greater than yours, knowing
that you have cooperated with God in the creation of
a new human being with a beautiful, tiny body and
an even more beautiful, immortal soul?

Yet, sadly, the world around us refuses to recognize
the beauty and wonder of motherhood. Today's society,
characterized by insatiable hedonism and materialism,
recommends raising "planned families"—typically two
children, spaced exactly two years apart—and main-
tains a hostile attitude toward Catholic mothers who
view motherhood as a gift, a privilege and a vocation
from God, and who remain open to new life throughout their marriage.

Catholic mothers endure the same difficulties as
other expectant mothers; they too experience bewil-
dering and uncomfortable changes to their bodies, to
their emotions and especially to their futures. They
feel just as sick, just as apprehensive and just as discouraged as other mothers. Dealing with these hardships without succumbing to society's distorted concept
of motherhood is not easy; Catholic mothers desper-

ately need spiritual guidance and support. Providing such guidance, encouragement and support is the purpose of the following reflections.

Unfortunately, there is not a lot of Catholic literature available today which specifically addresses the spiritual needs of an expectant mother. When I was expecting my first baby, I felt miserably sick for the entire nine months. Although I was eager to become a mother, I was surprised at how terrible I felt, and I was frightened about all the changes that were occurring within me. Since none of my friends was expecting at that time, I felt very alone. The people that I worked with were mostly my age or slightly older, but they were all waiting until they were "ready" to have a baby; even those who called themselves Catholic did not follow the Church's teaching on birth control.

I turned to my books, but there I found little or nothing. None of my prayerbooks had a single prayer for expectant mothers; my books on marriage and parenthood talked about the advantages of raising a large family, which was encouraging, but none of them ever discussed the challenges of pregnancy. Even the Catholic books on motherhood which I found rarely gave pregnancy more than a passing mention. This surprised me, for the Church encourages couples to have large families, so I thought there would be some Catholic resources providing spiritual guidance specifically for expectant mothers. After all, the mother of a large family spends a great portion of her life pregnant!

First-time mothers, especially, need a positive, spiritual perspective on pregnancy, or else they may be tempted to decide that their first pregnancy will be their last pregnancy. As the youngest of twelve children, I longed to have a large family, for I knew firsthand the joys and love that a large family can bring—but I was definitely discouraged about the means of acquiring a large family! However, after my first baby was born, and I knew the euphoria of at last holding and nursing my darling little girl, I began to write. I wrote to sort things out in my own mind: the seemingly interminable morning sickness and discouragement of the previous nine months, and the inexpressible joys I was experiencing in caring for a baby all my own at last. I continued to write during my next two pregnancies, and I found that I was helped immeasurably by identifying my own daily difficulties on paper and finding the spiritual solutions there as well. Although at first I wrote just to help myself, soon I realized that my writing could help other mothers too, who like me were seeking some spiritual guidance and encouragement on how to sanctify those joyful but trying months of pregnancy.

Pregnancy is such a personal thing that it is difficult to write about it in such a way that all mothers will feel that one is speaking directly to them. The same woman will tell you that during each of her pregnancies she experienced not only different physical symptoms, but different emotions and attitudes about her condition as well. After all, the thoughts and emotions of a woman during her first pregnancy obviously differ from her thoughts and feelings during her fifth or sixth.

The great variety of physical symptoms likewise poses a difficulty: one woman will vomit frequently throughout a very long nine months, while another will feel nauseated for three or four months, and a third will not experience any morning sickness at all. However, whatever the symptoms a woman experiences, each finds that pregnancy is difficult in one way or another; if a woman does not feel nauseated, she might suffer from backaches, heartburn or exhaustion; if a woman does not find her face, hands and feet swollen with water retention, she may notice her skin breaking out in a sort of acne that no teenager ever dreamed of!

Another woman will be afflicted with constipation and hemorrhoids. And there are women who suddenly find themselves diagnosed with various medical complications, which may cause some to be confined to bedrest for the last trimester, or restricted to an unbearably bland diet, due to gestational diabetes.

In addition to the variety of emotions and symptoms an expectant mother may encounter, a number of other situations can present unique difficulties. Maybe she has been trying to avoid pregnancy through periodic continence, because of serious medical or financial concerns; perhaps she feels anxious because her husband is opposed to having more children; or maybe she is not even married, but has conceived out of wedlock. This work will not cover all of these situations specifically; in fact, the attempt has been to address the typical Catholic mother under the most normal conditions. For example, at times I have referred to the expectant mother's husband or to her own joy over the news of her pregnancy. However, despite these occasional references, this work has no intention of excluding *any* expectant mother who may fall into a different category, and I believe that these reflections will somehow benefit *every* expectant mother, *whatever* her situation, in her efforts to recognize pregnancy and motherhood as her unique means of growing closer to God.

Another divisive issue that comes up occasionally in the following pages is whether a mother should seek employment outside of the home. This subject has become increasingly controversial in recent times, when so many mothers do work outside the home, for it involves the very core of one's concept of motherhood. That some mothers *need* to work outside the home for serious financial reasons is undisputed; however, in today's world, the working mother has become the norm, not the exception, even among Catholics—which shows how society has lost the sense of motherhood as a vocation, resplendent in blessings and abounding in grave responsibilities.

I realize that in addressing typical Catholic mothers, I am speaking to many women who plan to work outside the home after the birth of their babies, a few out of real necessity, but many for the sake of luxury, perceived as necessity. I make no effort in the following pages to offer arguments or to produce statistics to persuade the latter group to give up their jobs; this work is not an argumentative work, but a spiritual one. I hope only that mothers working outside the home who read this book may not be put off by any references to this difficult issue, but will prayerfully reevaluate their own reasons for working, meditating seriously on their vocations as mothers and requesting the light and guidance of Our Lord, who alone reads their hearts.

Already we have seen some of the great variety of symptoms and circumstances which color our perspective on pregnancy and motherhood. But whatever our situation, whatever our difficulties, we are all striving to learn more about our vocation as mothers and to learn how God intends us to achieve sanctity through this vocation; we are all striving to grow closer to Christ by fulfilling the duties of our vocation in the manner and spirit most pleasing to Him. No matter who we are, God sends us trials of various degrees and kinds, all meant to assist us in our journey to Him. May God grant that these reflections help expectant mothers understand how to use their trials to grow in holiness, virtue and love and to see their glorious vocation as mothers—with all its joys and challenges—as their path to union with Christ.

Contents

Prayers for Mothers

Your Labor of Love

A Spiritual Companion for Expectant Mothers

❧ 1 ❧

Love's Great Adventure

"Before I formed thee in the bowels of thy mother,
I knew thee: and before thou camest forth out
of the womb, I sanctified thee." (Jeremias 1:5).

MOTHERHOOD is a great adventure. Surely it provides all the excitement and uncertainty of any great adventure. True, there are tedious aspects to motherhood, but what adventure worthy of the name excludes hard and often tedious work? Consider the great Captain Cooke, who sailed the seven seas, exploring new worlds and charting unknown territory—did his long sea voyages entail no hard work, no tedium, no long months of patient waiting? The same could be said of the adventures of Marco Polo, Christopher Columbus, Daniel Boone, Davy Crockett, or any of the great explorers or adventurers. We could also say this of the great missionaries, such as St. Francis Xavier or St. Isaac Jogues. Surely their exciting lives had many hours of dull plodding, learning difficult new languages, waiting for wearisome journeys to end, and recovering from foreign diseases. Such moments, however, were sanctified by these holy men as opportunities to grow closer to God and to prepare spiritually for whatever lay ahead.

However, motherhood holds more excitement and wonder than the discovery of new worlds or new cultures. Motherhood is a discovery of the mystery of a new human being. Think about this for a minute. The baby within you has his own unique personality, sense

1

of humor, tastes, talents, ideas and even quirks! He will even have his own unique spirituality. He has an immortal soul and he will live for all eternity. You are co-operating with God in bringing this whole new human being into existence! Who knows what this child will be? Who knows the acts of love he will perform, the ideas he will bring to the world, the hope and joy and laughter he will have to offer? Now, and after his birth, you will be the one watching and guiding the unfolding and blossoming of this unique person.

One comment that parents of large families often hear is, "Each child is so different!" Obvious as it may sound, this observation can provide matter for meditation. Each child has something *unique* to offer within the family; each has a unique relationship with every other member, an ability to help the others in ways no one else could help them. Each has his own unique perspective. Likewise, each has his unique contribution to make to his society and to the Church.

One fascinating facet of the Catholic Church is her richness. While adhering always to unity in faith, she wisely offers a variety of devotions and spiritualities, each suited to attract different souls to God. Thus, every Saint has been unique and has had his own spirituality, suited to his own personality and temperament; each Saint has had his own favorite subjects for meditation, his own favorite prayers, his own unique contribution to make to the Church. For example, St. Philip Neri is known for his sparkling sense of humor, while St. Teresa of Avila is famous for her common sense; St. Thomas Aquinas is famous for his intellectual prowess, and St. John of the Cross for his lofty mysticism. As you can see, each Saint reflects the goodness of God in a unique way.

It is the same within the family, for the family is the Church in miniature, the domestic Church. Each member contributes his own thoughts, his own humor and his own insights to make the family a holier body. Your unborn child will have his own unique, unrepeatable contributions to make to your family. Many of these attributes are being formed right now; some will be taught to him by your example and the environment you create for him; others he will develop as he matures. But even though your example and your home will exert enormous influence on his young soul, he will react and respond to every stimulus in his own unique way. That is why motherhood is such an adventure: as we see our children's personalities unfolding, we are surprised and fascinated by the variety of responses and reactions to the wonders—and difficulties—of life.

Even in the womb, some babies reveal to their mothers glimpses of their own unique personalities; mothers have reported that some babies kick more than others, or kick in different circumstances. For example, some unborn babies kick when pressure, such as that of a seat belt, is felt, while others kick upon hearing music. With the technology of ultrasound, we know too that some babies suck their thumbs *in utero*!

Further, like each Saint, each child reflects the unlimited goodness of God in a different way. We know that a sunset reflects the beauty of God, and a thunderstorm displays His power, but we forget that each human being reflects His goodness and love in a far superior way, for each human being is made in His image and likeness—a boast that no thunderstorm can make! The beauty of your child's personality will reflect God like no sunset ever will. You are bringing into the world another true reflection of God's goodness, beauty and love. What a vocation! And *what an adventure!*

∽ 2 ∽

Discovering Pregnancy

"Behold thou shalt conceive in thy womb, and shalt bring forth a son; and thou shalt call his name Jesus." (Luke 1:31).

WHAT woman does not remember her feelings upon discovering that she was expecting a baby? At first, she is struck with incredulity, which gradually gives way to joy and excitement, not wholly unaccompanied by some nervousness or even a little tinge of panic . . . these are the emotions most often felt, under normal conditions. An observant husband may even notice an inner glow emanating from his wife in her joy—a glow that all too often and all too swiftly fades, drowned in a sea of morning sickness, weariness and mood swings.

The wise woman does not expect to retain this euphoria for the entirety of her pregnancy. She realizes that it is impossible to remain at such a high pitch of excitement for any length of time. Nevertheless, often she does not expect the gloom and discouragement that she experiences in the ensuing weeks; she may even feel guilty about not feeling happier about her condition.

It is foolish, of course, to feel guilty about not experiencing an emotion; emotions come and go and indicate nothing about one's intentions, one's thoughts, or one's will. However, it can be helpful, when absorbed in one's own discomfort, to reflect on the reasons why one is suffering thus, and what is being accomplished.

Think often about the tiny baby being formed inside

4

of you. Frequently call to mind your initial joy on discovering you were carrying this little life, and thank God for blessing you with one of His greatest gifts and privileges. The intense joy a woman experiences upon learning of her pregnancy, though it often vanishes quickly, impresses a memory upon her heart that will, with God's grace, be recalled frequently to help her through the difficult months ahead. Nine months seem like a long time when you feel nauseated and weary; when every night is a battle against heartburn and insomnia, and every day finds your growing body more awkward and heavy. But nine months is a very short time compared to eternity—for your child, whether he lives to be a day or a hundred years on this earth, is endowed with an immortal soul and is destined, with God's grace, to live forever with you in Heaven.

Never lose sight of the eternal destiny of the child within you, now and after childbirth, for this alone gives meaning to your vocation as mother, nurturer and teacher. Present discomforts and future sacrifices all fade in comparison to the privilege of helping to bring a new human being into existence, giving him the opportunity to make his own unique contribution to this world and enjoy the vision of God's beauty and love forever in the next.

⫷ 3 ⫸

Your Changing Body

"To the woman also he said: I will multiply thy sorrows, and
thy conceptions: in sorrow shalt thou bring forth children."
(Genesis 3:16).

EXPECTANT mothers quickly learn that God's
punishment for Original Sin is not confined to
the actual pains of labor, but often begins about
nine months earlier with nausea, tiredness, heartburn,
swelling, constipation, leg cramps, and a host of other
ailments, mostly minor but nevertheless annoying.
Morning sickness (a misnomer if there ever was one,
since it is rarely confined to morning hours) is perhaps the ailment most complained of in pregnancy.
Daily events that one used to take for granted, like
preparing meals, brushing one's teeth, swallowing vit-
amin pills or taste-testing baby food, can suddenly
become the most unpleasant moments of the day to a
nauseated mother. First-time mothers may wonder how
other women put up with these symptoms over and
over again. Others may become bitter and question
why God made pregnancy so difficult.

But here is an opportunity to appreciate the unique
beauty of the vocation to motherhood. A mother does
not simply give her time and energy to her vocation;
she gives her body, her very self. She gives until there
is no more to give. Nothing is spared. Every aspect of
her life has changed and will change even more once
the baby is born. In this she bears a remarkable resem-
blance to Christ. He gave us His Body when He died

on the cross. Every ounce of His Blood was shed for us. And He continues to give us His Body and Blood every day in the Holy Sacrifice of the Mass, as a mystical renewal of His Death on the Cross. Therefore, Christian mothers, do not deplore your growing discomfort, your disappearing figure, your changing life; you are in good company. With Christ, you are giving up your very body for love.

And to whom are you giving your body? Most obviously, to your baby, who so desperately needs the protection, security and nutrition that your body alone can provide. But also you are surrendering your body to God, who gave you your body in the first place. Prayerbooks often contain prayers such as, "O Lord, I give Thee everything I am and everything I have, all my earthly possessions, my body, my mind, my memory and my emotions. I entrust them all to Thee!" Perhaps we have seen these prayers without understanding their meaning; perhaps we ourselves have even offered such prayers to God. But now we can say this kind of prayer and truly comprehend its significance, for in pregnancy we surrender our body to Him in assisting Him to create a new life. Let us now offer our bodies to Him, again and again, to do with as He pleases, just as He so generously gave His Body up for us.

Remember, too, that the purpose of any vocation is to lead one closer to Christ and make one more like Him. You have just seen, in a small way, how the vocation of motherhood specifically can help you to do this. Resolve now, early in your pregnancy, to use every circumstance that comes your way, pleasant or unpleasant, to help you realize the purpose of your vocation. Everything from nausea, blood tests and hemorrhoids, to the tears of joy that rush to your eyes when you first hear your baby's heartbeat—all these things can be used to grow closer to Christ, for all these things are manifestations of love. Your sacrifices for your baby, however small, are akin to the sufferings that Christ endured for us; and your joys, however simple, are akin to the joy in Christ's heart when He encountered a loving or a penitent soul. Yes, in pregnancy—and, indeed, in all of motherhood—you will learn to love as Christ loves, sacrificially, but joyfully, for you rejoice in the fruit of your sacrifice.

Offer now to Jesus all that you will experience in your pregnancy, and ask Him to give you the grace to use each moment to grow closer to Him. Renew this offering every day until it becomes a part of the way you think, the way you react to situations; and slowly, over the period of nine months, you will learn the beauty and joy of your vocation, for you will be living your vocation as Christ intended. You will be living your life for love.

∽ 4 ∽

Challenges Unique to Your
First Pregnancy

"Perfect charity casteth out fear." (1 John 4:18).

A WOMAN'S first pregnancy is filled with unique joys, wonders and often also hardships. The knowledge that, for the first time, she is carrying a new life within her can be elating, fulfilling and exciting. The gratitude that fills her heart, so eager to love her child, can be overwhelming. Yet, the nausea, tiredness and other symptoms often discourage her in practical, everyday life more than she expected them to. Struggling to accomplish her daily work while feeling sick and tired, living on dreams for the future, is not easy. Further, because she has never had a child before, her dreams of maternity seem remote and unreal; only the morning sickness is real—all too real. What is she to do?

First of all, an expectant mother must be sure to get *lots* of rest. Minor problems seem insurmountable to one who is tired and low on energy. In a tired body, nerves grow taut, one's temper flares, and words are spoken which cannot be unsaid.

Right now, your body needs more rest than ever. Let the housework slide. You can attack it with greater vim tomorrow if you get to bed early tonight. Remember that the energy that you normally use to do a good day's work is now being diverted, not just to provide nutrition for your baby, but actually to form your baby's body. The formation of your baby's bones, organs and tissues is your most important job right now. Almost everything else can wait until you have taken your nap.

Second, focus on the cause of your joy—your little baby. When you have enough energy, browse through stores selling baby items. Not only will you have the chance to compare prices on baby furniture, but the experience will bring home to you the reality of the unborn life within you. Consider purchasing right away one or two baby outfits which particularly appeal to you, and take them out to look at whenever you feel particularly down or discouraged. Also, if you have even a shred of artistic talent, think about designing your own birth announcements; whether you use computer clip art, stencils, rubber stamps or your own original artwork, you will find this to be a fun, inexpensive way to focus on the joys lying ahead of you.

Last and most importantly, ask the Blessed Mother to accompany you at every moment of your pregnancy. Let her be your guide and companion. As you go about your daily duties, try to imagine how she would handle each situation that arises. Try to picture to yourself her appearance and her manner. There is a humble dignity about her, but also a great warmth and compassion. She does not put on airs, but eagerly seeks to help those around her who are in need, thinking nothing of her own inconvenience or discomfort. She derives the strength to act this way from her prayer life; not a day goes by that she does not meditate on Scripture and converse with God. Her relationship with God is intimate, personal and profound; to her, God is a real Father, all-wise and all-loving. She sees His tender care in everyday events; she sees His goodness in the simple joys of life; she speaks her thanks in the cheerful performance of her duties. Her home reflects the serenity and joy in her soul.

In all these things, Mary is your model; ponder how she lived and behaved, and strive to do the same. In all these things, she is also your mother and your companion; she regards you with the tenderest compassion; ask her for her aid. As your mother, as the Mother of mothers, she is uniquely able to help you. Like no one else, she understands what you feel: your blossoming love for your unborn baby, your daily struggles with morning sickness and weariness, your fear and uncertainty about childbirth and the enormous responsibilities that are facing you. She knows all these things. Pray to her—as a child, as a friend. She is your mother. She is the mother of Love Itself. She will strengthen your own love, for only love can conquer all your fears and overshadow all your discomforts.

Take Mary as your model and companion in your pregnancy. Allow the Mother of mothers to introduce you to your new and beautiful vocation.

∽ 5 ∽

Challenges Unique to Subsequent Pregnancies

"And his mother kept all these words in her heart."
(Luke 2:51).

P ERHAPS the biggest challenge for the expectant
mother who already has children is to remain
cheerful and energetic, despite the unending
amount of work that must be done. Women with children cannot take a day off, no matter how sick or tired
they feel. And woe to the woman who catches a cold
or the flu while she is pregnant, suffering double the
tiredness, but able to omit only a fraction of the work!
It is small comfort to say, "Oh, I feel sick; I guess I'll
skip the dusting today!" when meals must still be
cooked, little ones spoonfed, dishes taken care of,
laundry washed and folded, toddlers bathed, diapers
changed and teenagers counseled. There is no day off
for these mothers. After a long day, you cannot just
gulp down a bowl of cold cereal for dinner, curl up in
a chair and lose your lingering "morning sickness" in
a good book.

What makes your task most difficult is that all this
work must be performed with energy and good cheer.
Children are sensitive to your moods; even before you
lose your temper, they will sense your "let's-get-this-
over-with" attitude as you change a diaper, and they
will respond in kind. If you are living for naptime (if
all your children are still little enough to take naps),

they will absorb your unspoken impatience with them and will reflect it in their own way—in their own impatience with toys, with each other, with you—before you have time to rest your head in your hands and say, "Poor me!"

So, how does one act with enthusiasm and cheer when one's energy is at its lowest? With nature alone, it is impossible; you need supernatural aid. You must turn to the Mother of mothers, Mary. If you are "living for naptime"—or bedtime, as the case may be— you are denying your vocation. You are regarding your motherhood as simply a job, with so many hours per day. No wonder you have lost your sense of joy. The Blessed Mother will help you regain your perspective, to see the rewards of your vocation.

There are times when motherhood does not *feel* rewarding—toddlers become fussy or misbehave, older children go through annoying or even alarming phases—but the fact remains that your vocation, your privilege, is to form these souls as closely as possible in the likeness of Christ, to nurture them in their innocence, to broaden their horizons, to teach them to grapple with the world in which they live. The teenagers, as well as the toddlers, desperately need your consistent, cheerful and prayerful guidance. Your children are not just bodies to be clothed, fed, changed and entertained; they are human beings with immortal souls whom you are showing the path to Heaven. Once you regain your sense of fulfillment in caring for your visible children, how much easier to be joyful about the unseen life within your womb!

The rewards of motherhood are great, but like all good things, they are quickly forgotten in the everyday tasks and cares of life. The Blessed Mother is uniquely able to help you understand and appreciate your vocation. Whether or not you have developed a devotion to her in the past, now is a good time to get to know her better and to model your life on hers. She, too, had a household to manage, a husband to please, a Child to care for, and occasionally a sick neighbor to help out. Sinless but human, she surely had to deal with interruptions, lack of consideration from others, and many of the same little frustrations and heartaches that mothers face today. We can feel sure that she sometimes wept. But her glory is in the spirit behind her lowly actions: each was done out of love. For Mary's relationship with God was a personal, intimate and profound thing that encompassed every moment. In the little events that would occur each day, Mary could see God's Providential Will; in the simple joys of life, she could see reflections of His goodness; in daily duties cheerfully performed, she could see her own response as a loving daughter; in her motherhood, she could see the glorious opportunity to take part in her Father's work—to form and nourish, physically, intellectually, emotionally and spiritually, the Child given to her, who was God's own Son.

As you go about your day—fixing meals, changing diapers, scrubbing floors—picture to yourself how Mary would perform each action. When your husband comes home, notice the atmosphere that greets him as he walks through the door, and imagine the atmosphere provided by Our Lady for St. Joseph. However, Mary is not only the Model of mothers, but also the Mother of mothers. Pray for her intercession. Ask for her assistance. When the toddlers are wailing, the older children are bickering, the phone is ringing, dinner is about to burn and you feel as sick and tired as can be, remember that she is near to help you. Pray for her aid. She will never fail you. Make a practice of singing "Immaculate Mary" or some other Marian hymn when the day's work begins to oppress you; she will steady your nerves, lift your heart and give you strength always to see the beauty and glory of motherhood.

❧ 6 ❧

Bodily Discomforts

"Amen, amen I say to you, unless the grain of wheat falling into the ground die, itself remaineth alone. But if it die, it bringeth forth much fruit." (John 12:24-25).

HOW many times we have given up drinking coffee or eating sweets for Lent and patted ourselves on the back for our heroic sacrifice, and yet we complain unendingly about a trial that God has chosen to send us! We forget that often it is much more difficult to accept joyfully the difficulties that God sends us than to endure cheerfully the sacrifices that we impose on ourselves. For how often do we say, "Oh, if it were anything but *this!* I could take anything else, but not *this!"*

Pregnancy involves a variety of symptoms; no two pregnancies are exactly alike. But there is one similarity in all pregnancies: the symptoms are not of our choosing, but of God's. Accepting what God chooses to send us rather than choosing our own penances reflects the true Christian spirit, also known as the virtue of resignation to the Divine Will. This is truly a surrender of oneself to God, taking up the cross that He wills for you. Further, this is the essence of Christian perfection—conforming one's own will to God's will.

People often misunderstand what is involved in accepting suffering. It does not mean that you can never talk about what you are going through. Your husband, who has to live with you and deal with all your moods and vagaries, needs to know what you are

15

experiencing. Your mother or your doctor may be able to give you practical advice regarding certain symptoms. A sister or a friend may be able to offer you sympathetic support and thus strengthen you.

However, for those of us who are expecting, accepting suffering perfectly *does* mean that we must not grow bitter or angry about our trials; we must not complain about them constantly; and we must not allow them to make us short-tempered or irritable. Perfect resignation requires humility, patience and a spirit of obedience. It means recognizing God's wisdom as greater than our own. It means smiling when we have heartburn, remaining cheerful when we are tired, and praising God although we have just vomited. Frequent prayer makes this possible. As many times a day as you notice yourself complaining to yourself or others, or feeling sorry for yourself, repeat, "All for Thee, dear Jesus." You may not feel a surge of grace at that moment, but each time you offer your discomfort to Our Lord and sincerely try to cease even interior grumbling, He will shower you with grace and sustain you in your struggles. He will teach you to appreciate the value of suffering, while strengthening your endurance, until even the mounting pains of childbirth will be transformed into a *labor of love*.

∼ 7 ∼

Mood Swings

"For we have not a high priest, who can not have compassion on our infirmities: but one tempted in all things like as we are, without sin. Let us go therefore with confidence to the throne of grace: that we may obtain mercy, and find grace in seasonable aid." (Hebrews 4:15-16).

MOODINESS, loneliness and fearfulness are often experienced by expectant mothers; a few women may even endure some form of mild depression. Some of these emotions are caused by hormonal changes, while others are simply the woman's reaction to the many changes taking place within her. Either way, you can find relief and comfort, first, in realizing that you are not alone in your suffering; and second, in knowing that your suffering is not without purpose.

First of all, remember that Our Divine Lord Himself, in becoming man, willed to subject Himself to the emotional, as well as the physical, anguish which belongs to the lot of mankind. Thus He knew anxiety and fear as He lay prostrate on the ground and sweated blood the night before His Crucifixion, praying that this cup might pass from Him. Thus He knew loneliness as He repeatedly found His closest friends sleeping while He endured this agony of spirit in the garden. Thus He also knew the depths of human misery when He cried out from the cross, "My God, my God, why hast thou forsaken me?" (*Matt.* 27:46). Truly He felt abandoned by God, His Father, who permitted Him to

17

suffer such pain: not only the excruciating physical torments of His Passion, but also the almost intolerable burden of all the sins ever committed by man since the beginning of the world. Further, He foresaw that despite all of His sufferings, some of the souls that He loved so dearly would still be lost. Yes, Christ knew the very nadir of loneliness and human anguish, and as He watches you in your trials, He longs to comfort you and tell you that He understands—if only you will turn to Him.

Even more than this, He wishes to show you that your suffering has meaning and great worth. First of all, your tears and heartaches can be offered up for various intentions—the expiation of the temporal punishment due to sin, the conversion of a loved one, the end of abortion in this country and, most appropriately, the spiritual and physical well-being of your unborn baby. Remember, suffering is necessary to atone for our own sins and can also be used to make reparation for the sins of others. How blessed we are to have a chance, here and now, to shorten our stay in Purgatory and at the same time to offer up our tears and heartaches for those around us who ignore God and pursue all those amusements which sadden His Heart! Our tears, offered up with the proper spirit, will not be wasted, for they will move Our Lord to consider with greater pity those who have wounded and rejected Him, and He will shower them with more grace to incline their hearts toward Him.

Further, when we view with discouragement all the evil in the world, let us remind ourselves that to remedy these ills, we must first make reparation. We cannot end the evil of abortion by complaints, but by prayer, accompanied by mortification. If you really want to effect changes in the world, offer joyfully to God whatever suffering you experience. Similarly, the Church is the Body of Christ, and whatever you do as a member of this Body has repercussions on the rest of the Body; for example, when you sin, you weaken the entire Body, but when you offer up suffering joyfully, you contribute to the strength and health of the Body. So the next time you hear about a priest contradicting the holy teachings of the Church, or you see a Catholic college or institution promoting contraception or homosexuality, ask yourself if you are in any way to blame . . . have you been contributing to the health of the Mystical Body of Christ? Or have you been draining the strength of all the other members by your own sins?

Cheerful suffering goes a long way to remedy any harm your sins may have caused, and may also help atone for the sins of others! However, it may seem most appropriate and comforting to you to offer up your troubles for your unborn baby. Not only will your baby benefit from your cheerful offering, but you yourself will be strengthened and purified by these sufferings to become a better mother—a more selfless, patient mother. Remember, too, if your husband is not a practicing Catholic, it will be for the great spiritual benefit of your whole family to offer up your sufferings for his conversion to the Faith.

Our Lord does not like to watch us suffer. He feels more compassion for us than anyone else ever could because He loves us more—infinitely more. Nevertheless, He knows well how suffering, both physical and emotional, can help us to see the emptiness of the pleasures of this world and lead us to embrace a closer and more intimate relationship with Himself. Let us not waste this precious opportunity of growing closer to Him.

8

Making Friends with The Blessed Mother

"And Mary said: My soul doth magnify the Lord. And my spirit hath rejoiced in God my Saviour." (Luke 1:46-47).

PREGNANCY is a good time to grow closer to the Blessed Mother. Of course, we do not know exactly what Our Lady experienced when she was expecting Jesus; because she was free from Original Sin, she did not experience the pain of childbirth. We can be sure that she *did* experience a deep joy in anticipation, as well as a feeling of vulnerability such as every expectant mother knows.

Talk to Our Lady about your specific situation and about your expected baby. Ask her, "Is this how you felt when you were expecting Jesus? How did you feel when you first thought about the responsibility of caring for the Son of God?" So often we imagine Our Lady as unfailingly calm and serene, the way she appears in statues and on Christmas cards. We forget that she was human, that she was very young when she conceived Our Lord, that she had emotions, too. Even Christ, who was God, wept over Jerusalem and sweated blood in the Garden of Gethsemane; so also Mary, although without sin, experienced the full spectrum of virtuous human emotions.

Think for a moment about the impact of the Archangel Gabriel's announcement on Mary's life. Traditions tell us that as a child, Mary made a vow of virginity, and that at about age fifteen, in accord with God's Will, she took St. Joseph as her spouse, to support her and protect her vow. Otherwise, what could she have meant by her question, "How shall this be done, because I know not man?" (*Luke* 1:34). Our Lady's question makes sense only if she had already vowed her virginity. Consequently, there was nothing further from Mary's plans for her future than motherhood. Gabriel's message must have bewildered and confused her, for it drastically changed every idea she had for her future life; it almost altered her own identity, it gave her a new vocation. If you feel like pregnancy has thrown you for a loop, if you have difficulty adjusting to all the changes ahead of you—talk to Our Lady. She has gone through it. And she accepted her new vocation with wonder, humility and love.

Then, after the brilliance of the Angel Gabriel's light had vanished from her room, leaving Mary alone, perhaps the devil approached to tempt her with thoughts of false humility and fear. Was she not unworthy to become the Mother of the Saviour? Would not the life of the Mother of God be one of sufferings and trials? What would Joseph think when he learned of her pregnancy? But if Mary was assailed by unbidden thoughts such as these, she turned to God, repeating to Him that she trusted in His wisdom and love—and surely God rewarded her with the peace and serenity that comes from trusting in Him.

Pray to Our Lady that you may imitate her deep trust in God, which helped her to rise above fears; for she had to face her own share of fearful situations, as well as you do, but she also had the grace to overcome them. As a daughter goes to her mother asking what to do to relieve morning sickness, run to Mary—only you will be asking not only for physical remedies, but more importantly, for spiritual graces. She is your mother, your friend and your model as you embark on this beautiful phase of your life.

∽ 9 ∽

Your Great Work

"My bone is not hidden from thee, which thou hast made in secret: and my substance in the lower parts of the earth. Thy eyes did see my imperfect being, and in thy book all shall be written: days shall be formed, and no one in them."
(Psalms 138:15-16).

IN this ungodly world in which we live, filled with war, terrorism, abortion and so many other evils, a mother may be tempted to wonder why she is bringing a new life into existence; what has this terrible world to offer an innocent baby? And how much worse the conditions may be by the time her baby is grown up! When you grow discouraged by the evil world into which you are bringing your child, you may find comfort in the following reflections.

The life which is growing within you is not merely a human body, subject to sickness and death in this fallen world; rather, it is composed of both a body and an immortal soul, capable of the noblest acts conceivable—acts of loving God, praising Him and doing His Will. This immortal soul is destined, through the Sanctifying Grace of Baptism and with its own co-operation, to live in eternal happiness with God in Heaven. Thus, in co-operating with God's creative plan, you are involved in the sublime work of bringing forth one who will have the opportunity of participating in God's divine life forever.

Think for a minute about the significance of the little life within you. This baby will have his own unique relationship with God. The Sacraments were instituted by Christ with the salvation of your baby in mind, and when your child receives Holy Communion, his body will be a temple for the Sacred Body and Blood of Our Lord Jesus Christ. In fact, even after Baptism, this little body will already be a home for the Blessed Trinity, and will remain so as long as your child remains in the state of grace. So important is this little life that God will shower down upon it His graces and blessings, some of which your child will resist and some of which he will accept. If he perseveres in accepting God's graces, then this little baby will share in the divine life of the Holy Trinity for all eternity.

Remember also that this little life, whom you love so much, is loved even more by God. As precious as this baby is to you, he is even more precious to God, who created him, suffered for him and died for him. Yes, Christ died out of love for your little baby! Don't you feel closer to God for sharing a love for this child, whom most people don't even know exists? Don't you feel nobler for co-operating with God in the creation of a soul who will have the opportunity to praise Him and glorify Him for all eternity?

∽ 10 ∽

Tiredness

"Come to me, all you that labour, and are burdened, and I will refresh you. Take up my yoke upon you, and learn of me, because I am meek, and humble of heart: and you shall find rest to your souls. For my yoke is sweet and my burden light." (Matthew 11:28).

IN either the first or third trimester—or both—nearly every expectant mother experiences excessive tiredness. Although spiritual exercises may need to be modified to insure longer periods of sleep, do not make the mistake of omitting your prayer time altogether. Now, when you are weakest, you need Our Lord more than ever. Do not neglect Him, but rather, lean on Him, rely on His strength. His yoke is easy and His burden is light because He provides you with His strength to carry them. The yoke of the world is heavy because we must struggle along, using our own puny strength; but how great is our relief when we take up His burden instead!

Turn your weary, tearstained face toward Him. Tell Him about the housework you didn't get done, the dinner you burned, the sudden wave of emotions you feel. Lay these and all your troubles on His shoulders. See His compassionate eyes rest on you, His arms stretched out to comfort you. All He asks of you is to trust in Him. Give Him your troubles, rely on His strength, put down the problems that burden you and take up His yoke. Do not despair in your own frailty, but glory in it, for in your fragility you turn to God. You realize that you are weak, but you also realize that you do not need to be strong, so long as you have Our Lord to give you His strength.

Remember, too, that the irritability that you feel when you are tired is not a sin; this is a trial that you can use to grow closer to Our Lord. It shows you, once again, how weak you are; but although you may feel angry and impatient, these feelings are not sins in themselves; you commit a sin only if you give in to these feelings by speaking or acting impatiently, or if you dwell on your irritation in your mind, purposely indulging it. You may feel, at times, that you cannot go on without losing your temper or speaking sharply to someone. In a sense, you are correct; on your own strength you cannot. But remember, "I can do all things in him who strengtheneth me." (*Phil.* 4:13). Instead of giving in to your weariness, pause for a moment, close your eyes and tell God how irritable you feel, and ask His help. Rely not on your strength, but on His. Then go on with your work. It takes no longer than a second, but this little prayer will call down God's grace at a time when you really need it, so that, whatever inconveniences or annoyances confront you, He will give you strength to carry on—if not with a smile, then at least with calmness and inner peace.

Lastly, no matter how tired you are, do not neglect your prayer life. Prayer can be very difficult when we are feeling the nausea or exhaustion associated with pregnancy. We don't know what to say to Our Lord; we are too miserable to lift our hearts and minds to lofty things; we can barely think, never mind speak to our Creator! Sometimes we may make the supreme effort of kneeling by our bed for a moment, but it is only to recite listlessly a few memorized words before clambering into bed or going about the business of the day.

And yet by neglecting prayer, we are depriving ourselves of the source of our strength, which helps us persevere in our daily duties and which keeps us patient when we cannot sleep. But how can one pray when sunk in the depths of nausea, weariness and discouragement?

Remember that prayer is nothing but conversation with God. When you are feeling your worst, sit or kneel down, and simply tell God how you feel. Tell Him, in as much detail as you like, about the trials of mind and body that you are enduring. He is your Father and your Friend. He knows you and loves you better than you do yourself. He will not consider your tale of woe boring or insignificant; rather, He will value it as a precious token of your love and confidence in Him. Pleased that you have sought Him in your trials, He will bless you with the graces necessary to continue carrying your cross.

After you have finished unloading your mind, wait one more minute before collapsing onto your bed. Your mind is now clear, ready to receive the wisdom and peace God wishes to give you. Close your eyes and listen to God speaking in your heart. Perhaps He is only saying, "I love you!"—and yet how magnificent is this simple message, coming from our Lord and Creator! And how consoling, coming from our all-merciful Saviour! For if He loves us, what else matters? Listen to Him for a few moments and then respond, telling Him, not in empty phrases this time, that you love Him, that you regret having offended Him, and that you know He will be with you tomorrow, strengthening you every minute.

Now you may go to bed—and you will sleep better for it.

∽ 11 ∾

Worry

"And the Lord answering, said to her: Martha, Martha, thou art careful, and art troubled about many things: but one thing is necessary." (Luke 10:41-42).

WHEN you imagine the scene quoted above, do not think of Our Lord sharply rebuking the bustling, distressed Martha. He finds a need to teach her, it is true, but in the gentlest, most loving manner. Listen to His words. He repeats her name twice and then describes her as full of cares and "troubled." Clearly, He sympathizes with her, but goes on to show her how futile and unimportant her petty concerns are. Only one thing is important, one's relationship with God. Whether Martha will have dinner ready on time, whether she can prepare her special dessert, as well as fix dinner without Mary's help, are inconsequential. What matters is whether she loves God and strives to do His Holy Will. Mary, at the feet of Christ, is learning how to do just that. She has chosen the better portion.

Martha's bustle and distress over serving a perfect meal to Our Lord is quite comparable to the bustle and distress of an expectant mother on an average day. Pregnancy often brings tiredness, as well as other ailments, which deplete one's energy and make one irritable. Whether or not you are working outside the home, it is a struggle to find baby clothes, baby furniture, a pediatrician and a carseat, in addition to preparing a delectable dinner every evening and keeping the house clean. All of the preparation for the baby can be overwhelming at a time when you can barely manage to do the housework. Expectant mothers who already have children, of course, may have less shopping to do to prepare for their new baby, but they have more housework to accomplish and no more energy with which to accomplish it. Besides, shopping for new baby clothes might be easier than rummaging through closets, wondering where that box marked "0-6 months" went!

But Christ does not want us to become anxious and troubled about these things, because they are not essentials. The only essential thing is to love and serve God. Of course, serving Him involves doing one's duties as a wife and mother, trying to get dinner on time, unburned and appetizing, for example. But Jesus does not desire us to become overwhelmed by our duties; if we forget to take the casserole out of the oven and it is burnt to a crisp, we must not allow ourselves to become disconcerted—all we can do, at that point, is offer it up, knowing that what He desires is that we do our best and leave the rest to Him.

God knows that you feel sick and tired. This is His way of reminding you to get more rest, for within you, an entire new body is being formed. This takes an immense amount of energy, and your body desperately needs rest. Do not expect too much from yourself, and do not allow the piddling pressures of the day to undermine the peace in your soul. Hear Christ calling your name, as He did Martha's, and hear Him reminding you that your anxiety is needless. All you need to do is trust in Him. Scripture tells us, "Cast thy care upon the Lord, and he shall sustain thee." (*Psalms* 54:23). Put your cares into His hands. He will not drop them.

∽ 12 ∽

Fearfulness

"But Jesus turning to them, said: Daughters of Jerusalem, weep not over me; but weep for yourselves, and for your children. For behold, the days shall come, wherein they will say: Blessed are the barren, and the wombs that have not borne, and the paps that have not given suck."
(Luke 23:28-29).

PREGNANCY brings about a multitude of new fears and anxieties that many women have never thought about before. First-time mothers feel overwhelmed by the changes that have occurred to their bodies and feel anxious about the changes still to come. Some women worry about the health of their unborn child, especially if they have miscarried in the past. Some feel intimidated by the great responsibility lying ahead of them as mothers. Others simply fear the pain of childbirth. Even women who already have children may wonder how they will find time to care for another child—or they may worry about whether their upcoming labor and delivery will be as difficult as their last. Financial concerns may haunt others, especially those mothers who stay at home. Women who are expecting twins may wonder if they can handle caring for two infants at once. Although most of these fears are exaggerated, there is no guarantee that everything will turn out the way you want. There is only one solution to these fears—trust in God.

Remember, Our Lord is watching carefully over those faithful women who, with the Blessed Mother, have made their *fiat* to Him in being open to new life. Surely Our Lord's words to the weeping women on His way to Calvary can be applied to our own pagan times, when women trade motherhood for corporate careers or choose motherhood only when convenient—for example, after a house has been purchased and financial security has been established. In a world where so many women refuse to be open to His creative plan, Our Lord has a special place in His Heart for those few who accept the joys and challenges of motherhood on His terms, instead of on their own. Surely He will watch over these mothers in a special way, listening to their prayers and giving them the strength they need. He is never outdone in generosity. You have obeyed and trusted in Him; He will be with you throughout your pregnancy, strengthening you every step of the way.

Remember, too, that God does not give you the grace to endure the pains of childbirth—or whatever it is you fear—until you need it. He will not give you that grace today unless you are going to endure it today. But do not worry; on the day you need it, He will supply all the strength you need.

And if you are among those who did not accept motherhood on God's terms—whether you had been avoiding conception until you decided the time was right or whether you conceived "by mistake"—remember that Jesus spoke to the women of Jerusalem with compassion in His voice. Remember that He also spoke of great jubilation in Heaven over the repentance of one sinner. Knowing yourself unworthy, throw yourself on God's mercy. Trust in Him. He will not turn His back on you, but rather He will rejoice that you have finally come to Him. He will help you, too, through the difficult days ahead.

∾ 13 ∾

You Are Not Alone

"That you become not slothful, but followers of them, who through faith and patience shall inherit the promises."
(Hebrews 6:12).

WHEN you are feeling lonely, you may find consolation in becoming acquainted with some of the wives and mothers who belong to the Church Triumphant in Heaven. Reading their biographies, praying to them, imitating their virtues and asking them for their prayers may aid you in your spiritual life and console you in your hours of trouble.

You have many Saints from which to choose: St. Anne, the mother of Our Lady and grandmother of Jesus, is the patron saint of housewives and of mothers in labor. St. Felicity, we are told, was mocked by the Roman prison guards for crying out in pain while she gave birth to her baby in a prison cell. (Isn't it consoling to think that even a holy martyr did not bear childbirth in silence? You can see there is no need to be overanxious about appearing stoic before your husband and your doctor when you remember this Saint.) St. Perpetua, her companion, nursed her baby boy in prison while awaiting her martyrdom. St. Frances of Rome is famous for not letting anything, even her prayers, cause her to neglect her domestic duties; we are told that one day she was interrupted at prayer five times by household concerns, and each time she attended to the household problem without complaining, and then returned to her prayer. When she opened her prayerbook for the fifth time, the prayer she had been saying was written in gold. St. Dorothy of Montau lived a very difficult but heroic life with a wild, unloving husband (who eventually repented and converted) and with several sickly children. St. Bridget of Sweden brought up her eight children so piously that one of her daughters, St. Catherine of Sweden (also known as Karin of Sweden), was canonized as well. St. Elizabeth Seton was a wife, mother, convert and widow who educated her own children and others by founding a religious order. St. Margaret of Scotland helped her husband rule their country wisely and peacefully, so that she brought not only her immediate family closer to God, but her entire nation as well. Some women find Blessed Anna Maria Taigi particularly appealing because, unlike many other canonized wives, she did not enter a convent in later years, but spent her entire life ministering to her husband and seven children. And God has seen fit to keep the body of this humble housewife incorrupt.

Reading the life of Venerable Zelie Martin, the mother of St. Therese of Lisieux, may also be especially helpful because she led a very holy and yet very ordinary life as a wife and mother. Women with medical complications might pray to Blessed Gianna Beretta Molla, who was diagnosed with uterine cancer when expecting her fourth child and chose to die rather than abort her baby, who survived birth and is still alive today. Even more recently, Maria Corsini and her husband, Luigi Beltrame Quattrocchi, were beatified for their great example of Christian marriage and parenthood (three of their four children gave their lives to God as priests or nuns) and for courageously sheltering refugees in Italy during World War II. And there are many more wives and mothers recognized by the Church for their holiness, such as St. Rita, St. Elizabeth of Hungary, St. Monica, St. Sylvia, St. Hedwig,

St. Helen, St. Jeanne de Chantal, St. Matilda, St. Louise de Marillac, St. Elizabeth of Portugal, St. Margaret Clitherow, et cetera, for Holy Mother Church, in her wisdom, understands our need for models of married life and motherhood to help us along the pathway of sanctity.

Pray to these Saints. Look for their biographies. We will try to discuss as many of them as we can in this short work, but additional information may be useful to you. Remember that these women went through the discomforts of pregnancy, sometimes with a cold husband or unsympathetic in-laws; they wept when they felt sick or scared or lonely, and ultimately they found strength in Christ. Weep with them, talk to them, especially if you have few or no friends who have embraced motherhood at the same time as you. Then be sure to make friends with these women who have endured what you are enduring and who have triumphed in Christ.

∽ 14 ∽

Seeking Physical Comfort

"But the God of all grace, who hath called us unto his eternal glory in Christ Jesus, after you have suffered a little, will himself perfect you, and confirm you, and establish you."
(1 Peter 5:10).

WHEN a woman is feeling sick or suffering minor ailments of body or mind, it is all too common for her to seek consolation in pleasure, especially by eating too much junk food. An expectant mother faces even greater temptation to justify gluttony because friends tell her she is "eating for two." Furthermore, she may very well be experiencing unusually strong cravings, or if she is suffering from morning sickness, she must eat whatever food does not actually repel her. Of course, there is nothing wrong with satisfying a craving or enjoying good food, but an expectant mother is very vulnerable, and she must guard against seeking all her comfort in these fleeting pleasures and also be wary of developing habits that will be hard to break after the baby is born. The bottom line is this: if a woman's prayer life is strong, then her strength will come from God, and she will not feel the need to overindulge herself in physical comforts; if her prayer life is weak, then she will naturally turn to something—frequently, food—to fill the void within her.

A strong prayer life is indispensable to your spirituality and growth in holiness. Morning prayers, first of all, turn your attention to God from the very start of the day; a Morning Offering is especially beneficial, for in it, you offer all the work, sufferings and joys of the day to God, so that all that you think, say or do all day long becomes a prayer. For your night prayers, kneel down (if you can!) and go over your day from God's perspective; thank Him for any blessings you have received or goals you have accomplished; beg His forgiveness for any sins or imperfections you see in yourself; ask His help in all that is troubling you; and call down His grace upon your loved ones. Beginning and ending your day with God is crucial if you want to have any kind of relationship with Him at all.

However, this is not enough. If you want to grow closer to Christ, all the Saints agree you must spend at least fifteen minutes a day with Him, aside from morning and night prayers. This will fill the void in your soul. If you are not used to doing this, now is the perfect opportunity; pregnancy is a time of preparation, of spiritual renewal, as well as of great personal need. Try it. It is easy. The method most highly recommended is to find a good spiritual book—the Gospels, above all others—and read one section or chapter slowly and prayerfully. Any time you feel an inspiration to pray, stop reading and converse with Him who is always listening. When you have no more to say, continue reading in a like manner. If you feel no inclination to stop and pray, read the chapter again, even more slowly. God will see your effort and perseverance and will be more pleased with your continued attempts than He would be with the most eloquent prayers. If, over several days, you still feel unmoved, perhaps you could try another book. Not all spiritual writers appeal to everyone, and even different books within the Bible itself may move you in varying degrees at different points of your life.

This, my Friend, is the only antidote to the void in your heart; you can turn to food as so many others have done, but food alone will not satisfy you. You can turn to your husband, and he may help you, but even he cannot give what he does not have. He cannot take the place of the Infinite God in your life; only prayer, conversation with God, will truly lead you closer and closer to a more intimate, more deeply satisfying relationship with Christ than you have ever known.

◇ 15 ◇

Seeking Worldly Comfort

"That eye hath not seen, nor ear heard, neither hath it entered into the heart of man, what things God hath prepared for them that love him." (1 Corinthians 2:9).

WHEN you're feeling lonely or a little sick, you might be inclined to page through one of the many current magazines or books aimed at mothers which deal with the issues of bearing and raising children. There are many in the stores and libraries today. In fact, many expectant mothers are inundated with free copies of such books and magazines at their doctor's office; and you may hope to find a little companionship, light reading or useful information between their covers. However, be aware that even among materials which claim to discuss having children and caring for them, you will find a multitude of articles on limiting the number of children and working while someone else cares for them. Indeed, "family magazines" unashamedly display advertisements for various kinds of birth control, in addition to featuring articles on determining how many children one should have. Popular books on pregnancy and motherhood almost invariably include a discussion of the advantages of different forms of birth control, simply assuming that the reader wants to limit her children; these books also emphatically warn women that they may conceive again within a few weeks after giving birth, as if attempting to frighten young mothers unduly about a situation that does indeed occur, but only rarely, especially if the mother is breastfeeding. Some of these books try to scare their readers even more by claiming it is dangerous to conceive within a year of having a baby, which, as history shows, is only true if the woman has had severe medical complications. Furthermore, these books and magazines give "lip service" to stay-at-home mothers by talking about the importance of what these mothers are doing for their children—but, two pages later, another article will feature a discussion of how children thrive in daycare and how women who find fulfillment in their careers have happier children.

Although not all of the information offered by these books and magazines is harmful, it is unwise to make a habit of reading them because by having this type of material in your home, you are surrounding yourself with pernicious ideas. Remember, the more you become accustomed to lean on these books and magazines for emotional support, the more vulnerable you will be to their attack on your faith and your concept of motherhood as a vocation. Actually, the Church teaches that it is a sin to read books that endanger one's Catholic faith. Moreover, books and magazines which attack the Faith will only make you feel more lonely because you will realize how rare in today's society is a family with a truly Christian perspective.

Perhaps it seems a little fanatical to abstain from books and magazines on family life, of all things! However, we forget that Jesus called Satan "the prince of this world" (*John* 16:11); his evil influence permeates every aspect of this planet, even those aspects which purport to deal with wholesome family issues. But do not be discouraged at seeing the devil's power in this world. Remember that we are exiles in a foreign country, which has been called a vale of tears. We are not meant to be completely at home here. God implanted in our very nature a yearning for the infinitely Good and for everlasting life. Of course, this means we yearn for God our Father, and for Heaven, our true home. Do not be downhearted if you feel isolated or alone. Remember that complete and everlasting joy will be yours if you fight the good fight. Just keep your eyes on the goal, Heaven.

Sometimes Heaven seems very remote, like a dream that is too good to be true. To make matters worse, the way Heaven is portrayed in art and movies, it almost seems dull—although it definitely beats the alternative! In order to find comfort in the doctrine of Heaven, which Christ certainly revealed to us in order to encourage and comfort us, we must meditate on what Heaven really is.

Think about the best times of your life—the times when you were happiest, when you first fell in love, when you felt most fulfilled, when you had the most fun with friends or family, when you were most deeply struck with the beauty in nature. These are mere shadows of the joys of Heaven. Further, think about the greatest love you have known—the love between yourself and your husband, your love for the child within you, your love for any other children you may have. This love, which is the most precious thing to you in the whole world, is the best reflection of God Himself that we can know here on earth, for love is God's essence. God is love. And what do we do in Heaven but see more perfectly the God who *is* love, rejoicing in His beauty and goodness. That, indeed, is something to look forward to! As St. Paul wrote, "We see now through a glass in a dark manner; but then face to face." (*1 Corinthians* 13:12). Thus, the joys of this earth are mere glimpses—dim shadows—of the eternal joy of Heaven.

Even more, sometimes one may receive a foretaste of Heaven from graces of spiritual consolation that God gives, such as during prayer. But still it is true that "eye hath not seen, nor ear heard, neither hath it entered into the heart of man, what things God hath prepared for them that love him." (*1 Cor.* 2:9).

In the meantime, we can look for truly Catholic books and periodicals on family life which not only refrain from attacking the truths of the Faith, but actually strengthen us in our faith. These may help us while we are engaged in our spiritual struggle. Further, we can seek out other Catholic families through our parish or through local events, pro-life activities, etc. And, if we do occasionally read a more secular "family" magazine, we should not fail to write a concise letter to the magazine stating that certain articles or advertisements offend us, and charitably explain why.* (If the letter is published, who knows how many expectant mothers will read it! For many of them, it may be their first exposure to the fact that contraception is not only morally wrong but is also a serious threat to the happiness of their marriage—as well as a serious threat to their bodily health.)

But, ultimately, our relief must come from above. God alone will give us the strength we need to continue our fight, and He alone can fully comfort us when we are wounded. We must trust in Him: first, that He will sustain us in our exile; and second, that He will reward us beyond our furthest imagining once our battle is done. If we suffer for Him, even in little everyday things, He will grant us inner peace now and unending joy in the life to come. His generosity is never outdone.

---

* See Appendix II for a sample letter to a magazine concerning an advertisement for birth control. This may help you write your own letter in response to an article or advertisement that you may come across.

∽ 16 ∾

Praying for Your Baby

*"And fear ye not them that kill the body, and are not able
to kill the soul: but rather fear him that can destroy
both soul and body in hell."* (Matthew 10:28).

AFTER considering Heaven, it is only appropriate to spend time in the consideration of its alternative, Hell. It is truly amazing that we Christians spend so much energy worrying about future events, allowing images of momentary embarrassment or discomfort to torture our nerves, but we so seldom consider the greatest catastrophe of all—the damnation of our souls. Our Lord in the Gospel reminds us to worry less about the physical evils of this world which we know will end with death, and to concern ourselves more with the infinitely greater tragedy of losing our souls for all eternity.

In this, we must be concerned not only for ourselves, but also for those entrusted to our care, including the little baby that we carry this moment in our womb. We all want the best things for our children: health, happiness, a good education, a remunerative occupation, and a loving spouse, for example. But do we think about their eternal welfare? Do we consider the dangers lurking in the world which can destroy the morals we teach them, corrupt their innocence, and distract them from their spiritual life with all sorts of pleasures—moral and immoral? Terrible as it is to consider, your child will face during his lifetime the craftiest assaults that the devil can devise to lead him away from God. However well you teach and prepare your child for temptation, it is the choice of your child alone that will determine his eternal destination.

What can you do now, even before your child is born, to help prevent him from being hurled into unremitted agony for all eternity? More than anything else, you must pray. Pray for the soul of the baby whom you carry. Pray that God, in His mercy, will grant your child innumerable graces to strengthen him in times of temptation and at the hour of his death. In addition, offer up your current discomforts and difficulties for the eternal salvation of this baby whose body you protect, but whose soul is so vulnerable. Lastly, pray for yourself, that God may help you to teach your child and to form his mind so that he will appreciate spiritual things as more precious than the greatest wealth that the world has to offer; pray that you, with your husband, may bring to your home a peaceful, loving environment where your child may see his parents valuing the same ideals that they have taught him to value.

And what of yourself? Is it not wise to consider also the possibility of one's losing one's own soul? Of course. And again, prayer is the key. Prayer will keep us in the presence of God, ever mindful of *His* perspective on things, ever conscious of the pettiness of all worldly concerns, and the sole importance of the eternal. Prayer will strengthen you for your temptations and for your last hour on this earth. Likewise, your sufferings now will help you to see the vanity and foolishness of relying on earthly security and caring too much for those pleasures that end. Suffering forces you once more to turn to God, to ask for His assistance, to grow more and more in tune with Him. He carried a cross once for you, to save your soul from Hell. You must carry your own cross, too, in union with Him, so that His suffering for you will not have been in vain.

∽ 17 ∽

Marital Difficulties

"For the unbelieving husband is sanctified by the believing wife . . . otherwise your children should be unclean; but now they are holy." (1 Corinthians 7:14).

BECAUSE pregnancy often brings with it stress and great change, frequently it will aggravate any problems that you may already be dealing with, including problems between yourself and your husband. Although in this small book we cannot deal with all the potential causes of and solutions to marital difficulties, we can at least encourage and guide the expectant mother in her efforts to improve her marriage.

First of all, keep in mind always that you are not alone in your marital problems. Although some saintly women married saintly men and had very tranquil marriages, there are many canonized women who were married to quite the opposite type of man and encountered great difficulties in their marriages. In studying their lives, we can come to see how to deal with our own domestic problems. Prayer seems to have been the key for all of them. St. Rita was married to a rather wild man who met a violent death, but through her prayers, he converted before he died. St. Monica's husband was known for his terrible temper, and her neighbors were amazed that even in his anger he never struck her; prayer gave her the wisdom and patience to avoid confronting him while he was angry, but to discuss things calmly with him later. Blessed Anna-

Maria Taigi's husband was also fiery-tempered, but like St. Monica, she took no offense at his tantrums and tended dutifully to his needs, expressing no regret but only joy in her choice of a husband, who was at the core a good man. St. Elizabeth of Portugal suffered infidelity and unjust accusations from her husband, but her uncomplaining demeanor through her sufferings led her husband to realize her innocence and later to embrace the Faith as well. Through prayer, all these women found the strength to meet anger, injustice and unkindness on a daily basis with love and patience. Prayer, which is communion with God Himself, assisted them in their struggles with wounded feelings, anxiety for their marriage and their children, and deep loneliness. Recalling Christ's presence within their souls sustained them amid domestic strife, so that their husbands could not but be affected by their unwavering love and patience. Thus, prayer not only helped these wives through their difficulties, but led their husbands as well to a deeper faith and love. Their husbands may not have been canonized, but they lived better lives because of the example of their wives and strove to be more devout Christians, more considerate husbands and more loving fathers.

Of course, when discussing saintly wives, we assume that most of the problems were caused by their husbands; whereas, with ourselves, this is not necessarily the case! But whoever is the primary cause of problems in marriage, prayer is still the single most important factor in discovering the exact difficulty, in coming up with a solution, and in mustering the strength to apply the solution.

Another essential ingredient in a good marriage is communication with your husband. Most misunderstandings and hard feelings occur because of failure in communication. If your husband holds different views from you on some important topic or does something that bothers you, it is usually misguided to keep it to yourself and suffer in silence. Why? Because, unless you are already a saint, you cannot really suffer in perfect silence. Consciously or unconsciously, you will resent the lack of thoughtfulness or the difference in opinion; you may develop a "martyr complex;" and then you might lash out in other, unrelated ways, which perplex your husband, who has no idea that a problem exists. No, like St. Monica, you must seek opportunities to talk to your husband tactfully and lovingly; you may request that your husband refrain from an annoying habit that bothers you, or at least explain why you mind it; or you must let your husband know that you feel strongly about a particular issue and would like to discuss it. Harmony of ideas or habits may not come from a single discussion; but repeated discussions, done in a spirit of love and honesty, will bear great fruit.

Sometimes you will discover that your husband has better reasons than you knew for his actions or opinions; you must weigh them carefully to see if indeed he is not right after all. At other times, you will be overjoyed to see your husband, after some thought, alter his opinions to match your own. Often, both husband and wife will emerge with a broader perspective, as well as a closer bond uniting them. Of course, if your husband sees a need to correct you, you must be open to this type of communication, too; you may explain your reasons calmly, not defensively, and then apologize for any harm you may have done. If your husband approaches you less than tactfully, you should still try to react the same way, allowing him to vent, and then calmly explaining and apologizing. He probably suppressed his feelings, not wanting to hurt you, and then, when his resentment had built up to an intolerable level, he exploded. If you react calmly, he will feel safe in bringing such matters to your attention right away next time, instead of waiting until he can no longer speak about them kindly.

Even if we are not experiencing any particular marital difficulties, we should still pay close attention to our marriage during pregnancy. All too often, our physical discomfort and our growing bodies cause us to become self-absorbed, and our marriage may suffer, if only a little bit, as a result. We must always try to focus on the needs of our husband, sympathizing with any stress he may be experiencing over the upcoming birth, or any other problems at work or at home with which he may be contending. Also, we must remember that prayer and communication are essential not only to *solving* marital problems, but to *preventing* marital problems. Pray together daily, if he is willing; also, in your private devotions, pray for his spiritual growth; talk about issues honestly as they arise—*before* they become sensitive topics, if possible.

Further, even if our husbands have no obvious failings, like a violent temper, we must remember it is still our vocation as wives to help our husbands toward Heaven. We must look at our own example first; do we bear trials uncomplainingly? Are we patient when things go wrong, or do we allow annoyances to destroy our own serenity, and therefore, the serenity of the household? Are we diligent in performing the duties of our state in life? Do we provide a peaceful and pleasant atmosphere in our home? Do we expect our husbands to do more than their share of the household work? Do we express our appreciation for all that our husbands do for us? Do we talk to our husbands, tactfully but honestly, when something bothers us? Are we too embarrassed to talk about spiritual matters to our husbands? Do we, as wives and mothers, encourage our family to celebrate the Church's feasts with prayers and spiritual practices, or are we content to celebrate religious feast days in a secular fashion only? Have we consecrated our family to the Sacred Heart?

The Saints are our models and friends in our journey to Heaven. St. Rita, St. Monica, Blessed Anna-Maria Taigi and St. Elizabeth of Portugal can be special sources of inspiration to us because of their heroic examples of unfailing patience and unconditional love in their difficult marriages. Pray to them, that they may share with us their piety, their wisdom and their love, that we too may improve our marriages and lead our husbands closer to the Lord, who instituted marriage as a Sacrament and blessed us with our spouse: our lover, our companion and our best friend in our journey to Heaven.

∾ 18 ∾

Sleeplessness

*"In him was life, and the life was the light of men;
and the light shineth in darkness, and the darkness
did not comprehend it."* (John 1:4-5).

THERE are various religious communities all over
the world who roll out of their beds in the middle of the night, assemble in their chapels to
give praise to God, and then return to their cells to
sleep until morning. They do this for three reasons:
first, to ensure that God is glorified during all times
of the day and night; second, to show God that they
love Him more than they love their own comfort; and
third, to atone for all the sins that occur in the dead
of night.

Expectant mothers often find themselves getting up
in the middle of the night, too—sometimes because of
their all-too-frequent trips to the bathroom; sometimes
because they cannot sleep, due to their awkward shape
or to heartburn; and sometimes it is simply because
they have other children who always seem to have
nightmares on the very night that their mothers are
most tired! Whatever the cause of your sleeplessness,
you can change it from an annoying circumstance—
possibly even an occasion of sin—to a sanctifying experience, simply by your intention. As you rise from your
bed with an unconscious yawn, say to Jesus, "All for
Thee, O Lord." However sleepy you are, you certainly
can manage this simple prayer! And, if you are sufficiently awake, you might even add, "Praised be Jesus

49

Christ, now and forever!" with the intention of God's being glorified at all times, day and night.

If, on the other hand, you find yourself doomed to perhaps hours of sleeplessness, you will necessarily be more wide awake, and you will be able to say with more awareness, "O Lord, help me to fall asleep soon, if it is Thy will. Asleep or awake, I offer this time to Thee to comfort Thy sorrowful Heart for all those sins which are being committed tonight. I also offer my sleeplessness for all those tempted tonight, that Thou, in Thy mercy, might grant them the grace to be faithful; especially for all those women lying awake tonight trying to decide whether to have an abortion, and also for all those who will die tonight, that Thou wilt grant them final perseverance. Lastly, I ask that if I do not get adequate sleep tonight, Thou wilt grant me the grace not to be irritable or impatient tomorrow." Pray the Rosary for all these intentions. If that doesn't put you to sleep, then at least you are not wasting these valuable moments—moments valuable only to those who love God enough to see their value. If you still can't sleep, get up and read a book for an hour. But whatever you do, do it with the spirit of love, and God will reward you a hundredfold.

∽ 19 ∽

A Visit with Two Expectant Mothers

*"And Mary rising up in those days, went into the hill country
with haste into a city of Juda. And she entered into the
house of Zachary, and saluted Elizabeth. And it came to
pass, that when Elizabeth heard the salutation of Mary,
the infant leaped in her womb. And Elizabeth was filled with
the Holy Ghost."* (Luke 1:39-41).

WHILE meditating on the pregnancy of the
Blessed Mother, let us turn our thoughts to
her visit to her cousin, Elizabeth. Here is a
perfect example of two good women coming together
to encourage and to help each other in their new vocation. Although there is a great disparity in their ages,
they share a deep faith in God and the excitement of
approaching motherhood. They know that each of them
is playing a very special role in the plan of God. Imagine their holy joy as they sit together, sewing baby
clothes and discussing their plans, their anticipation,
and also their concerns. Did Our Lady express feelings of unworthiness about being the Mother of God?
Did Elizabeth communicate concern over being a good
mother at her advanced age? And did they not reas-
sure and encourage each other, one with the wisdom
gained through years of a life of faith, the other filled
with the wisdom that comes from being "full of grace"?
Perhaps they also talked about the words of the Angel
Gabriel, pondering their meaning. Perhaps they spec-
ulated on the role of Elizabeth's child, St. John the

Baptist, as the Precursor to Our Lord.

Above all else, each shared her joy with the other—the joy of anticipation. Elizabeth had yearned for motherhood for so long; now, her heart is filled with song, for when her dreams seemed most hopeless, God rewarded her trust with a son, a child specially chosen by the Most High. Nine months are nothing compared to the time she has waited already. And Mary—although motherhood is an unexpected and unsought privilege—has rejoiced in embracing God's will, in wondering at His mysterious wisdom, for He has made her consecrated virginity fruitful in ways that she never imagined. Not only is she to be the mother of a Son, but the mother of the long-awaited Saviour of the world and the Mother of God Himself! Further, she is to be the spiritual Mother of all of His followers until the end of time. What a glorious reward for her humble offering!

Your baby, too, has a special calling from God, a vocation known only to Heaven at this time. The Blessed Mother knows and cherishes your baby's special place in the plan of God. She has a special love for your baby. Thank her.

Elizabeth, at her advanced age, may not have had an easy pregnancy; Mary was there for three months to help her with the housework, to comfort her and provide companionship. Remember this, and when you feel tired or sick or moody, ask Our Lady to be with you and to help you through your difficult times as she did for Elizabeth. Ask her to join you at your bedside, in your kitchen or at your office, and to strengthen you. Ask her to share with you her wisdom, her patience and, above all, her joy, which will help you through these long nine months.

∽ 20 ∽

Jesus in the Womb

A certain woman from the crowd, lifting up her voice, said to Him: "Blessed is the womb that bore thee, and the paps that gave thee suck." (Luke 11:27).

THE words of the woman in the crowd vividly bring to our minds the reality of the infancy of Jesus. Like all other babies, Jesus relied totally on His mother to feed Him, to clothe Him, to bathe Him. God truly came as a real baby, and because of this Baby's utter dependence on His Mother, motherhood has forever after been raised in dignity and meaning.

We say that because God came as man, lived, suffered and died, now the life, suffering and death of every man has new meaning. The same is true for pregnancy and motherhood. By having been an Infant, totally dependent on His Mother, Our Lord has given new meaning to pregnancy. He knows of all the discomforts of pregnancy, and He makes use of them for the sanctity and salvation of many.

In fact, God used pregnancy as a part of His plan for the Redemption of mankind. He chose to become man, beginning with the very first and humblest stage of human life. We marvel at Our Lord's humility in coming to us under the appearance of bread and wine in the Eucharist; but in His Mother's womb, He was not merely unrecognizable, but completely unseen and unknown. Only Mary knew of His divine presence, and even she could not see Him.

Through Mary's maternity, Our Lord and Creator became man—enfleshed in a tiny body, resting snugly in His Mother's womb. Think of Our Lady's joy and awe, knowing that she was carrying the Incarnate God within her! Through your own maternity, a new human being is brought into the world, a new future follower of Christ, who indeed will become an actual temple of the Holy Spirit once he is baptized. While Mary carried Christ Himself, we pray that we are carrying future *Christ-bearers*, ones who will let Christ take over their lives until they can say with St. Paul, "And I live, now not I; but Christ liveth in me." (*Gal*. 2:20). And what of your own joy and awe, knowing that you are carrying one who bears God's image and likeness? Carrying one for whom He died? Carrying one whom He loves and one whom He longs to have with Him forever in Heaven, sharing His own divine life?

This, then, is the noble vocation to which you have been called, a vocation sanctified by Christ, who used pregnancy as the means to come into this world and save it. It is also the means God has used, from the beginning of time, to create new men and women in His image and likeness, and which He now uses to create new saints—"Christ-bearers"—for His Church and, ultimately, for Heaven. In our struggles with indigestion and diapers, let us not forget the beauty and dignity of this sacred vocation, rendered holy by the Son of God Himself.

∽ 21 ∾

Accepting Your Vocation

*"But he said: Yea rather, blessed are they who hear the word
of God, and keep it."* (Luke 11:28).

CHRIST'S reply to the woman in the crowd who blessed His mother can be a little disturbing. (See above.) At first it sounds as though He may be disparaging motherhood, or expressing ingratitude toward His own mother.* But neither of these attitudes would be consistent with the rest of His teaching. Therefore, what does He mean by His words?

Perhaps He is telling us what aspect about His mother, and about all mothers, is most precious in His sight. It was Mary's *fiat*—"Be it done unto me according to thy word"—that is most precious in His sight. It was Mary's *fiat* that proved her worthy. It is our obedience that makes us worthy. Mary's salvation came to her through being God's Mother, just as our salvation comes to us through our vocation as mothers. But what is it about motherhood that brings salvation? It is our acceptance of motherhood, with all its discomforts and sacrifices, that makes our souls beautiful to God. Christ was obedient unto death—reversing Adam's Original Sin of direct disobedience to God. Our Lady co-operated in His plan of salvation, uttering her *fiat*, her statement of absolute obedience to the Divine Will,

---

* According to Scripture scholars, the word translated as "rather" in this passage means something like "indeed also," instead of expressing opposition or contrast. —*Publisher*, 2003.

thus reversing Eve's Original Sin. We must follow her lead, making our *fiat* to God, accepting our new vocation and all that comes with it.

During pregnancy, concentrate on uniting your will more than ever to the Divine Will. Accept with joy the trials that God sends you. Try not to rebel against Him when you feel tired or sick or lonely, but ask Him for the strength to be among those blessed who "hear the word of God and keep it." For those who were not desiring to conceive, and thus found out about their motherhood with more dismay than delight, remember that it is never too late to accept, and even embrace, your motherhood. You have a greater challenge, but also a greater opportunity to grow in holy resignation, to acquire a spirit of obedience, and to learn how to trust in God. Meditate often on the infinite wisdom and goodness of God, who brings good out of evil and rewards those who have confidence in Him. Do not be weighed down by worry or feelings of guilt, but allow yourself to be joyful and excited about the precious, innocent life growing within you. Our Lord does not want us to be down-hearted or guilt-ridden; He wants us to confess our sins and then to start anew, which means accepting our situation and using it to grow in love and trust in Him.

But *how* can we accept sufferings with joy? By bearing in mind always that we are suffering for love— most obviously, for love of our baby: this new, innocent little person ensconced so securely in our womb. But we are also suffering for Jesus, our crucified Saviour. What can we give Him for all that He has done for us? Do not our cheerful offerings please Him and console His Heart, so saddened by the sins of the world?

The most powerful force in the world is love. You do not need to consider the great feats inspired by love that are recorded in history and literature; simply look around you. You see a young man giving up smoking cigarettes because the girl he admires objects to them; you see a pretty girl consistently wearing the color that she knows her boyfriend prefers, no longer mindful of her own preferences; you see the hard-working husband slaving away at a job which suits neither his talents nor his tastes, in order to support his growing family; you see the young wife raising her children far from family and friends so her husband can work at a job which fulfills him; you see the considerate husband displaying unknown sources of energy in running the household while his wife is incapacitated by childbirth or illness; you see the thoughtful wife rising early to fix her husband's breakfast after spending half the night rocking a sick child; at the end of marriage, you see many elderly men and women caring for their ailing spouses in their last illness or senility. In each of these cases, deeds which would never have been considered for a moment under other circumstances are performed without complaint or resentment because of the love that inspired them. Love has rendered these sacrifices easy.

If the love between a man and woman can be so strong, what then of the love of the Creator for the creature? What of the supernatural love between the Saviour and the redeemed? Do we allow the distractions and cares of the day to blind us to the reality of what Jesus suffered for us—freely, and out of love? Do we neglect His on-going presence in the tabernacle, perhaps only a few streets away, waiting for us to visit Him? He has showed us the tremendous power—the triumphant power—of divine love. If we truly love Him in return, then our inconveniences will be considered opportunities, our sufferings will be viewed as joys, and our work will no longer be toil, but a *labor of love!*

∽ 22 ∽

The Vocation of Motherhood

*"Yet she shall be saved through child-bearing; if she
continue in faith, and love, and sanctification, with sobriety."*
(1 Timothy 2:15).

MOTHERHOOD is above all a vocation. Bearing, nurturing, teaching and loving children is what best fulfills a woman's nature. The father will love his children, play with them and work hard to support them, but generally speaking, he will lose his patience if he has to take care of them on a daily basis. It is the opposite for a woman; separated from her children, she is preoccupied and distracted, wondering how they are and what they are doing. A woman thrives on providing the steady stream of love and affection that all children need.

With all this said, the mother's vocation is not easy. It means bodily discomfort during pregnancy, the pain of childbirth and the frustrations of a newborn's inconsolable wailing. The list of difficulties goes on and on. But dealing with the discomfort, the pain and the frustrations with Christian joy is what constitutes salvation for the Christian mother. This is her path to sanctity. This is her vocation.

It is such a temptation today, with so many mothers working outside the home, to think of motherhood as something one does "on the side," to consider the career that the woman pursued before motherhood as her true life's work. Mothers who stay at home, before as well as after giving birth, may feel useless because they are not earning money, and they fail to recognize the beauty and significance—and the difficulty—of what they *are* accomplishing. Their role as a mother is tremendously more important than any job they held before, and certainly not any easier. For mothers who do work outside the home, it is equally important for them to realize that their primary vocation is still motherhood; in a proper perspective, it is their outside employment that they are doing "on the side." It is their motherhood, not their job or career, which gives them their true identity and instills real meaning into their lives.

Mothers sometimes lack an understanding of the nature of their new vocation. Sometimes a vocation does not entail working eight straight hours a day; sometimes it means throwing up every morning. Sometimes it means sitting up all night with severe heartburn. In future months, it will mean getting up at odd hours to feed a crying baby. But co-operating in the creation of a new human life is infinitely more important than any job you ever had, because the fruit of this work is everlasting. Likewise, the formation and nourishment of a child, body and soul, are also infinitely more important than any outside job a mother may hold, even a job in a Christian organization which does great good for souls, because your primary obligation in life is the spiritual welfare of yourself and those entrusted to your care.

A mother's vocation is hard for the world to recognize because there is no set forty-hour work week, there are no brilliant corporate strategies, no heroic fights on a battlefield. But it is a vocation nevertheless, and a hard one. And also a beautiful one. Accept the discomfort of feeling nauseated along with the joy of feeling the baby kick—this is all part of your vocation. This is *your* path to sanctity.

∽ 23 ∽

Run-ins with In-laws

"Bear ye one another's burdens; and so you shall fulfill the law of Christ." (Galatians 6:2).

MARRIAGE puts us in a very odd position, for suddenly we find ourselves calling "family" people with whom we may have absolutely nothing in common, except for the love that we feel for the man whom we call husband and whom they call son or brother. Sometimes we are lucky and find ourselves feeling right at home with our in-laws, agreeing on everything from moral values to family customs to taste in clothes. However, all too often we may find in-laws to be a source of friction—not necessarily because either we or they are *wrong*, but simply because we are *different*. Young, inexperienced wives can feel threatened by the mother-in-law's domestic prowess, for example; whereas, more seasoned wives are annoyed by criticism of their own tried-and-true methods of home-making or child-rearing. Sometimes, announcing a new pregnancy causes that friction to vanish, at least temporarily, in the common joy over the new life. In other situations, announcing a pregnancy exacerbates the tension, either because our in-laws do not approve of our having another baby or because we feel that our in-laws are trying to interfere with our preparation for the birth, or our choice of names, etc. (It should be mentioned that this type of tension can occur even with our own families.) The last thing an expectant mother needs is more tension. How do we deal with this?

First, we must try to think well of our husband's family (or our own family, as the case may be). We must always give them credit for the best possible intentions, no matter what they say or do. Even if they are condemning our way of raising a family, we remember that they probably think that we would really benefit from doing things their way, and they are trying to help us. This does not mean that we have to do things their way, of course, but it does mean that we must avoid resenting advice given to us in a spirit of good will. Especially if they criticize us for having too many children, we must realize that they do not have a true understanding of Christian family life, and we should try, however we can, even if only by example, to give them a greater appreciation of family life the way God intended it to be lived.

If their criticism really seems unkind or malicious, then we must still regard them lovingly, remembering that the way they speak to us is often the way they think about themselves. This is almost always the case. People with low self-esteem or deep-seated dissatisfaction with themselves repeat to others the thoughts that they think about themselves; if they are constantly finding fault with others, it is because they are always interiorly finding fault with themselves. Thus they are generally quite unhappy with themselves, and they project this unhappiness onto others. On the other hand, people who are happy, secure and self-confident are quick to see the good in others; they tend to compliment and build up those whom they meet, using constructive criticism tactfully and sparingly.

So, rather than feeling angry or bitter against an in-law (or anyone else!) who habitually criticizes us, we should sympathize with him or her. Here we have a person who is most likely very unhappy with life or—more probably—with himself. Pray for him or her.

It is very hard to maintain anger at anyone for whom we sincerely pray.

Another way to overcome the friction between yourself and your husband's family members is to ask your husband to talk about them. Ask him about his favorite memories of various members of his family, especially those with whom you do not get along. It is hard to dislike anyone who has been kind to your husband or who holds a special place in his heart! Tell him the problems you are having with his loved ones, and ask him, too, why he thinks a particular person treats you unpleasantly; perhaps he knows of some situation, past or present, which would explain the attitude being displayed; or perhaps it is not that this person has any bad intent, but simply poor social graces! All these things may help you overcome your natural dislike and view each person in your husband's family in a loving, sympathetic way.

Lastly, try to put yourself in their place. Think how you would feel if the wife of your son or brother was having a baby, how you would want to feel included in all the excitement and plans. Let your in-laws know as much as you can to make them feel involved and special. If you visit, make the effort to be the one to show your husband's mother and sisters your ultrasound picture or describe to them your new stroller or diaper table, so that they will feel involved. If practical, try to ask advice on neutral issues, such as what features to look for in a stroller or carseat. Ask your mother-in-law, or your sisters-in-law, if applicable, about their pregnancies and their newborn babies. (Once your baby is born, remember to send or give them lots of photos!)

If problems with in-laws persist, pray to St. Elizabeth of Hungary, a queen whose in-laws ridiculed her and accused her of spending royal funds in her ministry to aid the poor and the sick. Further, when her husband died, they threw her and her children out of the castle and made it a crime for anyone to give her shelter! Few of us endure that kind of persecution from our in-laws, but still it helps to imagine how St. Elizabeth must have treated her husband's family while she lived at the castle and how she must have prayed for them and thought of them when they left her and her children homeless. Had she grown bitter or angry against them, she never would have been canonized; instead, she must have felt sorry for them, knowing that people who act with such cruelty must lack the joy and peace of God in their hearts. So, too, we must "bear one another's burdens" (*Gal.* 6:2), not complaining when we feel we have been wronged, but loving the unhappy souls who have hurt us.

As wives and mothers we should always bear in mind that our in-laws are here to stay, and there is nothing to be done but get along with them as best we can. Your husband is not responsible for the faults of his family, and you must not make *their* faults a bone of contention between the two of *you*. When an issue that concerns your in-laws arises, be sure to discuss it tactfully and honestly—and privately, so that you can always present a united front to both families. Avoid wrangling with or trying to change your in-laws; accept them as they are, pray for them, and deal with them as charitably as you can. Your husband will deeply appreciate your kindness toward his loved ones. Overlooking their faults, noticing their good qualities, and treating them courteously will raise you higher in his eyes than cooking a sumptuous dinner.

Fortunately, most of our in-laws are really good-hearted people; otherwise, how could they have brought up our husbands to be such wonderful men? Yet human nature recoils from anything or anyone unfamiliar, especially if we feel them to be threatening to ourselves and our own way of doing things. We must always try to empathize with our in-laws, making an effort to understand their perspective and their needs, giving them the benefit of the doubt, appreciating them for who they are, with all their strengths and weaknesses, and above all, treating them with the love with which Christ treats us.

∼ 24 ∼

Despondence

"Every one as he hath determined in his heart, not with sadness, or of necessity: for God loveth a cheerful giver." (2 Corinthians 9:7).

NO matter how much you wanted a baby before you became pregnant, pregnancy can be a depressing and scary experience. Loneliness often plays a big part in this. You alone feel a variety of new and unpleasant symptoms; you alone feel your emotions taking a roller coaster ride for no apparent reason; you alone face even greater changes to your body and to your life in future months.

One way to ease your loneliness is to confide in your husband. God has ordained the Sacrament of Matrimony such that He often uses your spouse as His instrument to speak to you or to help you. Let your husband know how you are feeling. Your husband cannot help you unless he knows what you are experiencing, physically and emotionally. Also, tell him concrete ways in which he can assist you, whether you need a hand with the dishes or whether you just want a big hug or a good cry on his shoulder. You may think he should know what to do without your telling him, especially if this is not your first pregnancy, but chances are, he feels helpless and frustrated watching you suffer. He needs to be told, lovingly and specifically, how he can make your life easier.

However, do not forget that the source of your joy is always God, though He works through your husband at times. Spending time with God in prayer every day will also console you. He is your Best Friend. Tell Him how you feel. He will fill you with His grace and will help you not to become overwhelmed by your trials.

Also, remember that doing things for others is the best medicine when you are feeling poorly. Your husband, who has been trying to give you his support, needs your love all the more. Be sure to thank him for his little acts of love and understanding, and be extra attentive to his needs in order to fight your own tendency to self-pity and self-absorption. The written word can be more powerful than the spoken word because it takes more effort; also, a written note lets your husband know you were thinking about him when he was not present. So write a little note of thanks every once in a while for the little things he does and leave it where he will be sure to find it.

Lastly, do not fall into the habit of complaining or whining. Be as cheerful as you can. If you cannot ignore your nausea or swelling, joke about them. Try to offer up your ailments to God for the souls in Purgatory, for the conversion of sinners, for mothers tempted to abort their babies, or for your own husband and baby, for whom you are most obliged to pray. Most of all, unite your sufferings to those of Christ on the cross, and suffer gladly for love of Him. Rejoice that He has given you this opportunity of making reparation for your sins and of giving back to Him a small measure of what He has given to you.

⫸ 25 ⫷

The Hidden Life

"And Joseph rising up from sleep, did as the angel of the Lord had commanded him, and took unto him his wife."
(Matthew 1:24).

WE know very little about the life of the Holy Family, and yet, what an endless source of meditation their hidden life should hold for those of us with families! We can begin our meditations on the time before the birth of Christ, when St. Joseph took Mary into his home during those joyful days of anticipation. How do you think life went on in that humble house, while the holy couple waited for Mary's time to draw near? Mary spent only three months with Elizabeth and Zachary; what were the remaining six months like? Try to imagine a typical day in your mind.

It is a small, lowly dwelling. Perhaps Mary is tired. She is about to prepare dinner, but first she sits down to rest for a moment. She can hear St. Joseph pounding his hammer in his carpenter's shop. Maybe the constant noise is difficult to bear. She picks up a piece of material lying in her workbasket. It is to be a garment for her Baby. She examines the stitches critically. How hard it is to sew such tiny sleeves! But she is determined that her Baby will have the best clothes that she can make; and though the material did not cost much, it will keep Him warm. She places the tiny garment back in her workbasket, and after a moment of prayer, she stands up, ready to prepare dinner.

A little while later, St. Joseph enters the tiny room, hot and grimy from a hard day's work. He can smell the pleasant aroma of dinner cooking, possibly fish, which is so abundant in that region, and he can hear Mary's sweet voice singing a Psalm, interrupted occasionally in her concentration over dinner. As Mary turns and sees him, she smiles and asks him if he has had a hard day. She pours him some water from a pitcher and tells him when dinner will be ready. But before sitting down, St. Joseph peers anxiously at his young wife, inquiring how she feels.

When dinner is ready, what is the conversation? Mary asks tactfully about the commission for a large table that St. Joseph is working on, and he answers quietly, telling her his difficulties with the task. Then he quickly changes the subject to her own condition: how has the day gone for her? Does she need any help with her work? (How he wishes he could afford to pay for some hired help! But this he leaves unsaid.) Mary answers cheerfully but truthfully; he is the head of the family and needs to know how she is doing. She knows he will use this information to take the best care of her. Lastly, both drift naturally into the subject of this new Baby, who already has brought them so much joy and peace. They wonder at God's goodness and perhaps speculate what this Baby will be like. They are excited, like other expectant parents, only their conversation is filled with references to God and His wonderful plans, which they are familiar with from their knowledge of the Old Testament Scriptures. As they finish dinner, Mary rises to clear the table, and St. Joseph helps her to remove the dishes.

Before we leave this peaceful household, let us present to our minds one more day of the beautiful, hidden life that goes on here. Have you ever envisioned the evening when Joseph brings home the news that they must travel to Bethlehem? As Mary quickly realizes that the journey must take place around the time that the Baby is due, she does not become alarmed or dismayed. She is not pleased at the news, of course; but she spends no time bemoaning the poor timing, worrying about her welfare or feeling sorry for herself.

Neither does St. Joseph. As head of the family, he knows it is his responsibility to take charge of the journey and provide for the needs of his wife and the Child, but he does not spend hours worrying or berating the government's decree, although he does spend hours in prayer, begging for God's assistance in this unforeseen circumstance. How does this couple, then, react to the news that might cause great anxiety and anger in other families? They look into each other's eyes, acknowledging their mutual concern and seeking the mutual encouragement that they know they will find there. Then, with one accord, they smile at each other. "Well, this is God's Will," one of them says, and they calmly begin making the necessary preparations. They know there is no such thing as "poor timing" in the Almighty Father's Providential care.

Just pondering these scenes brings such peace to one's mind! Mary and Joseph were a young Jewish couple, and although they had received the special vocation of a virginal marriage, they were nonetheless human, with joys and sorrows, happiness and heartaches, hopes and fears. What set them apart was their total union of heart and mind with God and each other. Their every action was an act of holy love, and their every thought a prayer. When difficulties or trials came, they immediately referred everything to God, their Father, praying over their troubles, discussing them peacefully and making decisions confidently. Within the family, each was always more concerned about the other. When one assisted the other, the latter expressed gratitude, appreciating the love behind the act.

It sounds simplistic, but how else can one describe their life together? And how else can we progress in holiness than by imitating their holy example in our own family life?

∽ 26 ∽

Interruptions

"Therefore, whether you eat or drink, or whatsoever else you do, do all to the glory of God." (1 Corinthians 10:31).

A S every mother knows, interruptions are a part of motherhood. As her children grow, the nature of the interruptions change—from diaper changes and feedings to trips to the potty and kissing scraped knees, and on from there—but the fact of interruptions never changes, and probably will not, no matter how old her children get to be, so long as she owns a telephone! This challenging and often frustrating part of motherhood begins, of course, before the baby is born, most noticeably with the mother's own increasingly frequent trips to the bathroom; other interruptions would include frequent trips to the kitchen to refill her glass of water, so that she does not become dehydrated; trips to the doctor, as well as naps she must take when, due to her condition, she feels exhausted. Of course, a mother on forced bedrest finds her whole life has been interrupted for a few weeks or months. Insignificant as some of these interruptions may be, St. Paul tells us to sanctify everything we do— no matter how trivial—and certainly interruptions are no exception to the rule. Besides, if we realize that these types of interruption serve as a preparation for the more numerous interruptions that we will encounter after the baby is born, then we can see that it is important to train ourselves to respond properly to these annoying, but potentially sanctifying, occasions.

When we are deeply absorbed in a task, it is exasperating to have to stop to do something else; often it seems that interruptions repeatedly come at the most inconvenient moment possible. Sometimes we may wonder irritably how we are expected to get anything done when we are so often interrupted? Even more frustrating is the situation of those of us on bedrest, who must watch day after day as our household chores remain undone or are done by others in a way we would not do them. But then we must stop to ask ourselves, "For whom am I doing this task? Is it for myself, or for my husband and family? Is it for myself, or for God?" It makes sense, if we are doing our work for our own sake, that we should become angry if we are interrupted, for our plans have been thwarted, even if only for a few minutes. However, if we are doing our work for our husband and family, it does not make sense; for surely we are working for their well-being or their pleasure, and how does it increase their well-being or pleasure to live with an irritable, resentful wife and mother? And it makes even less sense to become upset over interruptions if we are doing our work for God, for His plans *cannot* be thwarted. He knew of this very interruption from all eternity and allowed it to happen. Evidently, He would rather have us deal with this interruption at this moment than have us finish the task at hand which seems so important to us. And if we are trying to serve Him, who are *we* to determine *how* we serve Him, so long as we please Him?

In short, when we allow ourselves to become upset at interruptions—or actually at any annoying circumstance—we reveal the impurity of our intention. We are not really working to please our husband or children; we are not really working to please God; we are working only to please ourselves. Once we realize this, we can accept interruptions as part of our day's work and all as part of our day's service to our family—and above all, to God.

St. Therese, the Little Flower, would not even finish dotting an "i" or crossing a "t" if the convent bell rang or another nun came to summon her to some other duty. She wanted to render perfect obedience to God, and she knew that He was commanding her through the convent bell and through her superiors. Unless we work at a school, it is unlikely that we will have either a nun or a bell summoning us to meals or Holy Hour or recreation. Nevertheless, if we imagine that it is God's voice summoning us when we are interrupted at a seemingly inopportune moment, perhaps we will resent the interruption less, for we will see it as an opportunity to serve Him. Think for a moment of how eagerly we would view an interruption if we were expecting an important phone call, perhaps from our husband. How quickly we would lay down our work! How much more quickly we should lay down our work if Our Lord is calling on us to do something for Him!

Interruptions seem like little things, and yet how often we allow them to alter our mood! We blame them for our failures in our work, and we allow them to make us irritable, sometimes even frantic, for the remainder of the day! We let interruptions destroy our interior peace. Yet if we can conquer our own will in these little things, how much easier it will be to conquer our will in the bigger things! And, in the not-so-distant future, how much easier it will be to treat a wailing infant, a restless toddler or a moody adolescent with love and tenderness when we realize that it is not just they, but Our Lord Himself who is asking us to put down our work and tend to their needs.

∞ 27 ∞

Alienation

"If the world hate you, know ye that it hath hated me before you. If you had been of the world, the world would love its own: but because you are not of the world, but I have chosen you out of the world, therefore the world hateth you."
(John 15:18-19).

U NFORTUNATELY, Christian mothers may feel alienated by the society around them because of advice that they receive which contradicts their faith or because of outright criticism or ridicule. First-time mothers may remember hearing others advise, "It's much better to wait a year or two before having children—you need some time alone together." Expectant mothers who already have children may be met with, "You're going to have *another* baby! When are you going to stop?" or "Another one so soon?" (The raised eyebrows can be harder to bear than the direct criticism.) All too often, even those friends who do not criticize still do not understand and do not sympathize with the difficulties in being faithful to Christ. In addition to social alienation, Christian families often face financial struggles in an economic system which almost necessitates two incomes per household.

To make matters worse, Catholic individuals and organizations frequently promote the use of Natural Family Planning, the practice of abstinence during the times of the woman's fertility, neglecting to make clear that the situation a couple is in must be sufficiently grave to render such an extreme measure morally permissible.* Pope Pius XII, in his Letter to Midwives, gives four general reasons when periodic continence is permissible: for serious reasons of the medical, economic, eugenic (e.g., great likelihood of producing severely handicapped children) or social order (e.g., disruption of life from war, earthquake, etc.).

However, many Catholic couples today use Natural Family Planning with a contraceptive mentality, and often Catholic institutions wrongly encourage them to do so. This fact only adds to the alienation that a Catholic mother may feel when she strives to be truly generous in her openness to new life instead of "planning" her family. (Before doctors discovered ways to determine accurately the woman's actual fertile days, the only completely reliable and licit way to prevent conception was total abstinence. Because total abstinence involves such great sacrifice, couples usually did not resort to this means unless there was a truly grave reason. However, since periodic continence involves abstinence only at certain times, couples tend to use it more readily, even when there is really no serious need. This is against the constant teaching of the Church, including the encyclical *Humanae Vitae*, and it contributes to the contraceptive attitude of today's society.)

Surrounded by such a contraceptive culture, Catholic mothers may sometimes doubt themselves and their adherence to the Faith.** They may be tempted to

---

*According to Catholic teaching, the correct term is actually "periodic continence" (cf. *Cat. of the Cath. Church*, 1997, no. 2370), where—for a proportionately grave reason, and only for the time that this reason exists, and only with the free consent of both partners to the restrictions involved, plus where the practice is not an occasion of sin to either person, especially the sin of incontinence—the couple uses only the infertile time in the woman's cycle to come together, though always leaving the avenue open to new life, if God chooses to give them another child. (Cf. Jone, *Moral Theology*, Imprimatur ✠ John J. Wright, D.D., 1961; TAN, 1993, no. 760.) —*Publisher*, 2003.
**To remind oneself of God's view of the serious wrongfulness of birth control, one should read and meditate on *Genesis* 38:1-10, where God slays Onan in the very act of practicing a primitive form of birth control. —*Publisher*, 2003.

agree that a year of married life before pregnancy might have been pleasant, or that their budget would be a little easier to balance with fewer children. (Certainly their waistlines could have used a few more months to lose the extra fat from their last pregnancy!) They need to be reminded that love is naturally fruitful; it longs to grow and spread and spend itself entirely. Normally, a spouse does not need all the love and undivided attention that you have to give. Children alone can fill up that vacuum; they *hunger* for that love which overflows from your heart. Love is generous by nature; how can the love of a couple be unselfish if it shuts out the possibility of new life? How can their love be genuine if it refuses to accept the fruit of their union?

Further, how can marital love be real when it accepts only part of the spouse, rejecting the other's life-giving capacity, which is so fundamental to each other's identity as man or woman? How can marital love be true when it accepts the lover conditionally—so long as the possibility of conception has been satisfactorily ruled out? Birth control, in claiming to make love *free,* has actually made love *false*, for true love accepts and embraces the other, with all the other's powers and potentials, especially those most fundamentally belonging to the other as a man or woman. True love knows no conditions. True love is unselfish, generous and fertile. Further, true love does not foster mutual selfishness; rather, true love wants the best for the other, and thus, true love seeks to develop the virtues of selflessness and generosity in the other because these are two of the greatest possessions that the other can attain.

Couples who hesitate to have another baby because they worry about depriving the children they already have of certain monetary advantages should remember that the best gift you can give to your children is not a roomful of video games or all the latest toys or gadgets, or a college education, or a sizable trust fund in the bank; no, the most valuable gift you can give your children is the gift of a baby brother or sister.

How do children benefit from this gift? Living in a family with a number of siblings is like taking a course in human nature; with each additional sibling, children learn better to understand others' perspectives, to deal with others' quirks and vagaries, and to get along with various personalities. Guided properly by their parents, children with siblings learn to share, to help others with their various needs, to speak to people on different levels, to communicate when conflicts arise, to tolerate others' faults, and to forgive offenses against themselves. In short, in learning to live together in the society of the family they are simply learning to love. They learn, like St. Paul, to become "all things to all men, that I might save all." (*1 Corinthians* 9:22).

Not only that, but in each new sibling your children will likely find a lifelong friend. Neighborhood companions and schoolyard playmates rarely display the loyalty and understanding of a brother or sister, even during childhood; how much more rarely do these friendships last throughout one's life! However, your children will have their family for the rest of their lives, and each child will grow close to different members as they pass through different stages and gradually mature. What a comfort for them to have a friend from their childhood, who thoroughly knows them and shares their background! Such friends can understand and help each other as no one else can. What can be a more valuable gift?

The fanciest toys and gadgets are the ones of which children tire most easily; the games that provide the most fun are those that are played with their imaginations. Later, when they are older, your children can find part-time jobs to help pay for their own college tuition, if necessary, and if they go to college. Often, they learn to appreciate their education more when they pay for all or part of it themselves. However, they cannot buy another brother or sister; they cannot pay to have learned how to love and help others each day as they learned to tie their shoes and say their alphabet. Thus, genuine love for your children provides no obstacles, but only more reasons, for being open to new life. Once again, we see that true love is naturally fertile; it encourages generosity and selflessness in others, as well as in ourselves; it knows no boundaries, no conditions, and thinks nothing of its own needs and comforts.

To understand this concept more clearly, consider God, who is Love. (*1 John* 4:16). His love is certainly fruitful. From all eternity, the love of the Father begets the Son, and the love between the Father and the Son brings forth the Holy Spirit. Here we see the fruitfulness of Love in its purest form. In addition, God decided to share His love further by creating man— and who can count the millions and billions of souls that He, in His divine generosity, decided to create, and for whom He died? If we are to be godly women, then we must imitate God by loving truly, generously and unconditionally.

∽ 28 ∽

Bearing Saints

"But the servant of the Lord must not wrangle; but be mild towards all men, apt to teach, patient, with modesty admonishing them that resist the truth." (2 Timothy 2:24-25).

IS it not truly remarkable how many saintly women have had saintly children? Of course, common sense tells us that this is not a coincidence; rather, the wise and holy training that saintly mothers give their little ones leads them to become saints as well. Let us think about this for a minute.

It is often said, "You can't give what you don't have." Therefore, if you do not have the makings of a saint within you, how can you pass on to your children those practices and attitudes that lead to sanctity? If you already have children, then you know that little ones imitate everything they see their elders doing. You may tell your toddler every day to be patient, but if on a regular basis he sees you lose your temper while fixing dinner or while performing some other chore, then chances are he will never learn the virtue of patience you are trying to instill in him. So, for your child's sake, you must become a saint so that he will have the best opportunity of becoming one, too.

However, every child has been given the gift of free will. He is free to accept or reject the truth that you present to him. Therefore, we cannot overlook the importance of prayer. Recall again St. Monica, who was married to a pagan husband. Surely she gave her son, St. Augustine, the best religious training that she could (although she wasn't able to have him baptized), but still he rebelled and lived a sensual, pagan life. As you may know, she persevered in prayer for eighteen years before her son converted, and God rewarded her for her persistence by giving her son not only the gift of faith and Baptism, but by leading him to become a bishop, and eventually a canonized saint and Doctor of the Church. God also gave Monica's husband the gift of faith and led Monica herself to sanctity.

Another mother to keep in mind is Venerable Zelie Martin, the mother of St. Thérèse of Lisieux. After being told by a Mother Superior of the Visitation nuns that it was not God's will for her to enter the convent, Zelie determined to become a wife and mother and raise saints for the glory of God. From then on, she prayed that her children might become saints. Was it a coincidence then that all five of her children who survived childhood consecrated their lives to God as nuns? We know that it was not only the way Zelie reared her children but also her prayers that led to this result, since Zelie died when her youngest child was only four, and it was this child who has been canonized and even named a Doctor of the Church. What a glorious response to Zelie's humble petitions! It seems that God was pleased with her prayers. It is reasonable to think that, realizing her imminent death, Zelie offered much of the sufferings of her last illness for the sanctity of her children, whose formation and upbringing she was unable to complete. Thus we see the value of suffering, of offering Our Lord our prayers and tribulations—however big or small.

We have a tremendous duty to our children, to raise them in the manner most conducive to their sanctity; and because we all are fallible, we have a tremendous duty to pray for ourselves. We must pray that we ourselves will know when and how and where to discipline, to praise and to teach our children for both their spiritual and psychological well-being (for the two are closely linked); but since every soul is endowed with free will, we must also *pray* that our children will be open to accept God's will for them, that they correspond to God's grace and that they live and die in His grace.

Obviously, this whole process can be started right now. By turning your attention to your own spiritual progress, you can help ensure that your unborn child has a worthy teacher; by praying and offering your unsettled digestion and swollen feet to God, you can trust that the All-merciful Lord will guide and protect your precious child.

⮞ 29 ⮜

Bitterness

"Let women be subject to their husbands, as to the Lord:
because the husband is the head of the wife, as Christ is
the head of the church. He is the saviour of his body."
(Ephesians 5:22-23).

IT is unfortunately common today to hear women express anger at men because men do not have to endure the discomforts of pregnancy or the pain of childbirth. Even good-hearted mothers, when feeling depressed or sick, may be tempted to develop a bitter or even a superior attitude toward men, whose lot, they imagine, is free from hardships. However, this attitude is unfair and uncharitable toward men and rebellious toward God, who designed and ordered our nature according to His infinite wisdom.

First of all, men cannot help the fact that they do not bear children, nor should they be blamed for not wanting to, since no one likes pain, and most women themselves would escape all pain, if it were feasible. Certainly men do not wish this pain on women, though they may wish for the fruit of that pain, children, as do millions of women themselves.

Secondly, we should remember that when Eve was condemned to bear her children in pain, Adam was also given a punishment: as the head and leader of the family, the curse laid upon him by God was to labor to support his wife and children by the work of his hands and the sweat of his brow. This is no light responsibility! While the mother spends her energy directly on her loved ones, cooking their food and washing their faces, the husband toils at his work outside the home— in an office, in a factory or in a field—where he meets with all the petty injustices, backstabbing, dishonesty, foul language and moral pollution of the outside world. Often he is forced to do work that does not appeal to him in the least, but will pay the household bills. He does not see the efforts of his hands directly benefiting his family each day; this happens only indirectly, once a week or twice a month, on payday. True, this role suits his nature better than the daily care of children, but that fact does not make his role easy or pleasant, just as your inborn maternal instinct does not wipe away morning sickness.

Today's mother oftentimes tries to assume the responsibility of financial support as well, pursuing her career as ambitiously as any businessman. This is not only contrary to her nature, but foolhardy, for she is seeking an additional burden which Our Lord had intended to spare her. No doubt this woman feels justified in berating man's "easy" lot, for she is *choosing* to bear both her punishment *and* his!

Of course, in this imperfect world, occasionally a family's economic situation necessitates the mother's working outside the home, but both husband and wife should remember that this is not the natural order of things. When a working mother experiences the stress, guilt feelings and frustration that comes from working outside the home, it is false charity to tell her that combining motherhood with a career is necessary for her fulfillment; rather, telling her that she is bearing more than her natural share of work will enable her to understand and to deal with her own frustrations and difficulties, as well as to help her to work toward the true solution. In such a case, there is no reason to feel guilty over a situation which cannot be prevented. However, these situations are more rare than one might suppose, and should not be mistaken for the norm, as is done so often today. In the meantime, the feelings of guilt that the working mother experiences as she kisses her little ones goodbye every morning, and the exhaustion she experiences on encountering a stack of soiled dishes after putting in a hard day's work at an outside job, can be offered up to God: first, for the formation of her children, whose training she is unable to oversee directly; and second, for a viable alternative for her working outside the home. Oh, the working mother has great opportunities of growing in holiness if only she understands her situation as it is, accepts it and offers it up with love to God. May she never lose sight of her true vocation, which is to be a wife and mother!

When mothers, whether at home or at an outside job, identify themselves and their vocations with motherhood, they find it much easier not to become embittered by the sufferings involved in pregnancy and childbirth; they learn to recognize these trials as a difficult but beautiful part of their life's true work. Thus, rather than embittering them, the suffering expands their hearts, making them more loving, more understanding and more compassionate toward *all*, both men and women, who bear the punishment due to Original Sin.

∽ 30 ∽

A Long Wait

"And behold I am with you all days,
even to the consummation of the world." (Matthew 28:20).

MOST expectant mothers find it hard to wait for the pregnancy to be over, either because they yearn for relief from the discomforts of pregnancy or because they are so eager to see their newborn baby. Mothers who are confined to bedrest during their pregnancy may have an especially difficult time with patience. However, it is not wise to pin all one's hopes on a future event or to postpone one's happiness until a later date, for then you are living as if your happiness depended upon human events rather than upon God. God is our joy. He alone is the source of our strength, our peace and our happiness. God wills that we be equally peaceful during our trials (such as nausea or bedrest) and during our blessings (such as your first embrace of your newborn baby). This may sound contradictory, as we have often urged the reader to focus on the reality of the baby and his impending arrival, for this keeps up our courage and our hope. However, we must not allow ourselves to concentrate so much on the future that we grow to think of the present as a miserable condition that we barely tolerate, believing that we are merely *surviving* pregnancy and that we shall start to *live* again once these hardships are over and the baby is born. No, we must learn to truly *live* our pregnancy, joyfully and expectantly, and to appreciate each stage that we experience.

How can this be done? First, you must realize that you do not become a mother when you give birth; *from the moment you conceive, you are truly a mother*, loving your baby, praying for him, and doing whatever is best for him, although you cannot yet see him, except briefly on the ultrasound screen! But even the great joy of motherhood can be ephemeral and elusive, sometimes tinged with worries; we need something even more profound, more concrete, to carry us through pregnancy. In short, we need the Infinite God. We need to focus more on Him than on ourselves and our own ups-and-downs. For instance, when we pray, do we spend more time discussing our problems or meditating on God's goodness? Of course we should tell Our Lord what things we need and what things we find difficult, but the prayer should not end there. Once we have unloaded our troubles, our minds are free to receive the light and peace and wisdom that come from *listening* to God. As in any friendship, we cannot do all the talking. Learning how to pray and really converse with God is where spiritual reading, which has already been mentioned, especially comes into play.

Here are four efficacious ways to help move the focus from yourself to God, which can supplement your daily spiritual reading.

First, remember throughout the day that, as long as you are in the state of grace, the Holy Trinity, God, is dwelling within you, and in any free moment you can speak to God within you, and He will hear you. This thought so greatly moved Blessed Elizabeth of the Trinity that she would be perfectly recollected and focused on God's presence within her even as she did her work around the convent, for example, sweeping the floor. Of course, had she two or three toddlers on her hands, I think the story might have been a little different! Nevertheless, in the few brief moments of quiet that come in a mother's day, whether it be while washing dishes or trying vainly to fall asleep, you can pause to remember the Blessed Trinity within you and to thank God, in awe and wonder, for His condescension and His love.

Second, develop a strong devotion to Our Lord in the Holy Eucharist, which is indeed the most concrete and tangible proof of His love that He has given us. If at all practical, make an effort to visit Our Lord in the Blessed Sacrament; or if you cannot, then at least pray to His Eucharistic Heart and make a Spiritual Communion each day. (This simply means asking Him, since He cannot come to you sacramentally, to come to you spiritually. Most Catholic prayerbooks will supply you with a formula to say for a Spiritual Communion, but you may also make up your own.) Meditate on His patience in waiting in all the tabernacles all over the world for men to seek Him and find comfort in Him. When you are able to attend Mass and receive Holy Communion (whether daily or weekly), do not begin and end your preparation and thanksgiving a few minutes before and after Mass; rather, begin your preparation the night before, telling Jesus how much you are looking forward to receiving Him tomorrow and asking Him to help you receive Him worthily and devoutly. When you rise the next day, remind yourself that today will occur the most important event of the day or week: you will be receiving the King of kings and Lord of creation in a most intimate and personal way. Not because of your own presumption do you go to receive Him, but because, on account of His great love for you, He longs to come into your heart and draw it closer to His own! Then, when you go to church, you will be better prepared for the wonderful Sacrament that you are to receive. Similarly, that evening, in your night prayers, thank Our Lord again for the grace of having received Him, and ask Him to continue to nourish your soul with His grace until you can receive Him again.

Third, meditate often on Christ's life, whether by reciting the Rosary, making the Stations of the Cross, or simply reflecting in your own mind. (A decade of the Rosary can easily be said while standing in line at the grocery store or sitting in the waiting room of the doctor's office—sometimes you may even get in all five decades, or more! Carry a Rosary around with you, or a Way of the Cross pamphlet. This is also a great way to evangelize if anyone sees you and asks about it.) Think of His birth and infancy in light of your own motherhood; think of His Passion in terms of your own current suffering; think of His Resurrection as bringing salvation to yourself and your little one.

Fourth, in addition to your daily fifteen-minute session of spiritual reading, try to read Catholic magazines or the lives of the Saints in your free time. There is nothing like reading about the amazing mortifications and accomplishments of the Saints to put your own life and your own priorities into perspective!

In these ways, you will keep your thoughts focused on the supernatural. This will bring joy to your pregnancy and indeed to your whole life.

❧ 31 ❧

The Approaching Birth

"And she brought forth her firstborn son, and wrapped him up in swaddling clothes, and laid him in a manger; because there was no room for them in the inn." (Luke 2:7).

AS the birth of the baby approaches, even experienced mothers may feel a wave of panic sweep over them. The inevitability of the pain of childbirth suddenly hits home. Uncertainty about potential medical problems also arises. Some women become anxious that they will need an emergency C-section or that their baby will not be healthy. Others know they need a Caesarean section and dread the operation, as well as the recovery period. Some women worry about making it to the hospital on time. As our fears threaten to disrupt our peace of mind, let us turn once more to the Blessed Mother.

Can you see her, on the back of the donkey during the long journey to Bethlehem, fatigued after a long day of traveling, feeling a little nervous about giving birth to her Baby in a strange city, far from family and friends? We do not know exactly which of the discomforts of pregnancy she may have experienced, although she would not have suffered the pains of labor since she was never under the influence of Original Sin. But we can form ideas about certain things she did experience. We can sense her discomfort as St. Joseph leads the donkey through the crowded streets, from one inn to another, perhaps losing his way a few times. Darkness falls, and we can imagine her heart sinking as each innkeeper, one after another, turns them away. Some are probably sympathetic; some are probably rude. Perhaps Mary is too tired to notice. We can only guess at her feelings when she finally realizes that she will give birth to the King of kings in a stable inhabited by animals. But once more, she turns to the Lord in prayer, and soon she is filled with wonder, praising the omniscient God for His mysterious ways. Then, aloud, she assures St. Joseph that they will be perfectly comfortable here and points out to him that the manger is the ideal size for the Baby's first crib.

Like Mary, you must learn to trust in God. Childbirth is a natural process; the pain you experience, though intense, is not the same sort of pain one feels when one's body is being injured. Nevertheless, all pain is scary to our human nature. And uncertainty over medical problems can be very distressing. But God will give you the strength you need. He does not give it to you now—because, unless you are going into labor as you read this, you do not need it now. When the time comes, He will help you.

Put yourself in the care of the Mother of mothers. She knows your fears and uncertainties; she too had to walk in darkness on many occasions. But she knew how to trust in God, to give Him all her concerns, and she will show you how, also. Give your fears and worries to Mary, tell her about them all, and then be done with it. She will take care of you, she will be with you during childbirth and will watch over you and your little one during those critical hours. Put yourself in her hands, and you will have nothing to fear.

∽ 32 ∾

Discouragement

"He shall feed his flock like a shepherd: he shall gather together the lambs with his arm, and shall take them up in his bosom, and he himself shall carry them that are with young." (Isaias 40:11).

DO you sometimes feel frightened? A little lonely? Do you think sometimes that your "morning sickness" will never go away, or do you feel overwhelmed by other ailments, worries, or perhaps medical complications? At times do you feel so discouraged about your pregnancy that you just want to sit down and cry?

I think all expectant mothers, especially those in their first pregnancy, sometimes feel these various emotions. Strangely enough, sitting down and crying often makes us feel better. However, it is good at these times, while we are crying, and particularly on those days when we cannot cry, to call to mind the scene that the Prophet paints for us of the Good Shepherd (cf. *Isaias* 40:11 above); note that He gathers the small lambs up to His bosom and He Himself carries those who are with young—the expectant mothers. There is a definite emphasis here, showing His gentle, almost preferential, care for these mothers in their blessed and yet very vulnerable condition. Yes, toward those of His flock who are co-operating with Him in the creation of new life, He shows a special gentleness, understanding and love. He approaches our weak, fainting hearts with a tenderness and compassion that we have never encountered before. The purest love between spouses and the most unselfish love of a mother for her child are dim shadows of Christ's love for us.

Further, in carrying us, He is not merely treating us with extra gentleness, but He is leading us where we need to go. For surely, blinded by our nausea, our weariness and our discouragement, we need guidance more than anything! And this the Good Shepherd provides for us. He watches over us, He knows our capacity for hardships, and He sends us trials which He knows are not so heavy as to break us, but which will rather bring us closer to Him, if we use them properly. And when we, dazed by the onslaught of the difficulties that confront us, reel back in bewilderment, He is there, supporting us with the strength to endure, enfolding us in His arms. We do not need to understand why this trial was chosen for us; that is His role as our Guide and Shepherd: to choose those trials which will strengthen us and best prepare us for Heaven. But also, as our Shepherd, He shows us how to deal with these trials and gives us the strength necessary to persevere.

Remember above all, when you are feeling discouraged, that you are not alone. Christ, the Good Shepherd, is tenderly carrying you—not only understanding your pain, but also offering you His help in bearing it. The Good Shepherd will never desert His flock, nor will He forget those mothers who have accepted His sacred and wonderful gift of life.

∽ 33 ∾

Imitating Christ

"Whosoever will be the greater among you, let him be your minister: and he that will be first among you, shall be your servant. Even as the Son of man is not come to be ministered unto, but to minister, and to give his life a redemption for many." (Matthew 20:26-28).

A WISE mother will meditate often on this Scriptural passage, both before and after she gives birth, for her vocation involves serving her children in many capacities. This passage will apply more obviously to a mother after she has given birth, for she feeds her baby, wipes his mouth, bathes him and changes his diaper, thus serving him in a most intimate way. Some mothers may see these duties as tedious or even degrading and pass them on to a nursemaid or daycare center, while they follow a career they consider more lofty or more challenging. But what is more noble than an act of love? What is more lofty than imitating Christ? What requires more careful precision and skill than forming the mind of a young child? Remembering the scene where Christ washes the feet of His Apostles, a mother bathes her own child with greater humility and love.

Likewise, before giving birth, you are already serving your child. You feed your baby with the food you eat; your womb provides the baby with warmth and security. You please your baby with the songs you sing. By taking good care of yourself, you protect your baby. With every step that you take, you are carrying your child and bearing his weight. By suffering nausea, tiredness, swelling and constipation, you sacrifice yourself for the baby's well-being. Already, you are serving your baby in a most intimate way, supplying your baby's every need.

Truly, before giving birth, you are imitating Christ by serving the needs of another. As your tummy grows and your center of gravity shifts, you may feel clumsy and sluggish. But despite your increasing awkwardness, do not feel embarrassed, for your awkwardness is due to your beautiful vocation as mother, servant to those you love, in imitation of Our Lord Himself, who served us by giving His very life to redeem us. He, too, looked awkward—bearing His heavy cross, falling under the weight of it in front of a jeering crowd. The blood and sweat dripping into His eyes prevented Him from seeing clearly where He was going, and His feet must have tripped several times from sheer exhaustion. And yet, there is great beauty in this scene, where God Himself stoops to such a level of suffering and weakness in order to serve the souls whom He loves. Likewise, we too should bear our own weaknesses—tiredness, moodiness, awkwardness—in our love and service for the little one who needs us, and we can ask for no greater Model in our task.

❧ 34 ❧

The Privilege of Parenthood

"And they brought to him young children, that he might touch them. And the disciples rebuked them that brought them. Whom when Jesus saw, he was much displeased, and saith to them: Suffer the little children to come unto me, and forbid them not; for of such is the kingdom of God. Amen I say to you, whosoever shall not receive the kingdom of God as a little child, shall not enter into it. And embracing them, and laying his hands upon them, he blessed them."
(Mark 10:13-16).

JESUS truly must have loved children. We can be sure of that from the way mothers brought their children to Him that He might simply touch them; we can see it in the children's faces, shy but attracted, in wide-eyed wonder; we can hear it in His voice, tender and gentle toward the children, but stern and indignant toward those who would hinder them. Again, we hear His protective anger when He says, "And whosoever shall scandalize one of these little ones that believe in me; it were better for him that a millstone were hanged about his neck, and he were cast into the sea." (*Mark* 9:41).

Our Lord's love for children extends to those whom He has created but who have not yet been born. It extends, therefore, to the little life growing so rapidly in your womb. What a privilege, then, that He has entrusted to your care one of His little ones! Today, people think of parenthood as a right to be demanded at the exact time and situation of their choice. Some decide to have one boy and one girl and then quit

95

(often by means of sterilization), as if they were ordering products from a catalog. If a couple cannot have children naturally, often they will go to any length, however unnatural, to claim that "right"—even to such extremes as *in vitro* fertilization. They forget that parenthood is not a right, but a privilege and a blessing from God. He is granting us stewardship over His beloved children. He has loved each child so much that He has willed to bring him into existence from nothingness, and He has desired that each child be exactly as He created him, with his own unique personality, talents, inclinations, strengths and weaknesses. Then He gives the child into the care of two parents, who, all unworthy, have the awesome responsibility of guiding, teaching and forming this child, so that he may live a life pleasing to his Father in Heaven.

Remember that your primary job as mother is to prepare your child for eternal life. This child is "yours" not in the sense that you own him; he is "yours" in that you are his caretaker, his role model and guide during a crucial part of his sojourn on earth. This truth, far from separating you from your child, actually brings you closer to him. Everything which is solely of this world ends with death, but your relationship to your child, ordained by God and nourished by grace, will have eternal ramifications. For all eternity, your child may bless you for being the first one to turn his childish soul toward his Lord and God, and to encourage his youthful heart to yearn for the unending joys of Heaven.

❧ 35 ❧

A Process of Love

*"For I was hungry, and you gave me to eat; I was thirsty,
and you gave me to drink; I was a stranger, and you took me
in: naked, and you covered me: sick, and you visited me:
I was in prison, and you came to me. Then shall the just
answer him, saying: Lord, when did we see thee hungry, and
fed thee; thirsty, and gave thee drink? . . . And the king
answering, shall say to them: Amen I say to you, as long as
you did it to one of these my least brethren,
you did it to me."* (Matthew 25:35-37, 40).

TOWARD the end of pregnancy, most of the initial excitement has vanished. The symptoms that at first we thought we could handle so easily are beginning to wear us down, and the thought that we still have a while to go discourages us. "Why does God make pregnancy so difficult?" we ask ourselves impatiently. First-time mothers, especially, often wonder why God makes pregnancy so *long*? What we fail to see is the true nature of pregnancy. We get so bogged down in the daily cares and troubles of our lives—our growing bodies, our increasing awkwardness, our shortness of breath, our frequent trips to the bathroom, our less than flattering appearance (and perhaps even our lingering morning sickness that everyone said *should* be gone by now)—that we neglect to recognize that pregnancy is, in essence, a process of love and our own unique path to Christ.

From the very first moment, pregnancy is, indeed, a process of love, for it begins with one of the most sublime types of love known to us—the love between a man and a woman. For, to the Christian, the marital act does not involve the self-seeking, insatiable, lustful passion that the world associates with sex; rather, the marital act is a true expression of the love of the husband and wife for each other; the marital act is a generous and unreserved gift of self, a true self-surrender of each to the other, out of love. Pleasure, of course, is involved, but each spouse primarily seeks the pleasure of the other—thereby most effectively insuring his or her own satisfaction in fulfilling the true meaning of what they are doing, making *love* to each other. Thus, it is God's plan that in giving their bodies completely to each other, generously and without reserve, a couple begets and conceives a new life, a life that is to be the fruit of their union, the fruit of their love.

Once the pregnancy is discovered, the love grows even more, for there is another person to receive love. However, the mother may not realize that she is, indeed, giving love to her baby, especially if she is not the sentimental type. After all, it is difficult to *feel* any love for a person one has never seen or met, a person who remains completely unknown, often even in gender! Here let us remember what Christ said to the doubting Thomas: "Because thou hast seen me, Thomas, thou hast believed: blessed are they that have not seen, and have believed." (*John* 20:29). If we substitute the word "loved" for "believed," then we see that those who love without *seeing* the object of their love, without *feeling* the fulfillment of their love, without *experiencing* the rewards of their love, are also blessed in God's eyes. For love is not a feeling; it is an act of the will. And in loving this baby with all of her will, although the baby is completely invisible and unknown to her, a mother is loving in a much higher, nobler way than perhaps she has ever loved before. In another passage, Our Lord says, "Love your enemies . . . . for if you love

them that love you, what reward shall you have? Do
not even the publicans [do] this?" (*Matt.* 5:44, 46). He
is extolling a truly unselfish love that seeks no earthly
reward. To love without earthly reward is to love as
God did when He who was perfect and lacked nothing
sent His beloved Son to earth to save the miserable
creatures who had offended Him.

Once we truly learn to love this baby, whose smiles
we do not see and whose cooing we cannot hear and
whose tiny fingers we cannot touch, then we suffer
joyfully, out of love, for the sake of this baby. We are
loving as Christ loves, neither seeking nor tasting
any reward. We see our sacrifices as little or nothing, and our work—preparing the nursery, buying baby
clothes and appliances, and then washing them, and
finally, the ultimate work of giving birth to our precious infant—all this work becomes, no longer a burden, but our *labor of love*. We suffer and we work,
not in resentment or bitterness or self-pity, but in the
joy of our motherhood. We cannot see or hear our
child; we can only feel his legs kicking on occasion;
but we love our baby, we glory in his unseen presence in our womb, and we wait patiently until that
miraculous day when we will see him, hear him and
hold him in our arms.

For the day will come when you first cast your eager
eyes on your baby's face, when your baby's tiny fingers will wrap themselves around yours, and your baby's
sleepy eyes will open slowly and gaze in wonder at
your joyful face. Then the hardships of pregnancy, the
pains of childbirth, and the challenges and sleepless
nights still to come all melt away in the joy of bringing into the world a new human being, created by God,
entrusted to your care, endowed with a unique personality, a beautiful smile and an immortal soul. You
will be the one to awaken and form the child's spirituality, his love of God and of neighbor, his virtuous

habits, his intellectual curiosity, his sense of security, love and fulfillment.

From now on, your life is different. Your nights do not belong to you, for you rise every few hours to feed the hungry. Your days are no longer yours, for changing diapers, washing soiled crib sheets and baby clothes, and constant feedings take up most of your time. Eventually, the feedings and diaper changes grow more spaced out, but now other responsibilities lie in waiting. Your meals are not your own, for you spend mealtime jumping up and down, cleaning spilled milk and wiping sticky fingers; your leisure time is not your own, for as soon as you sit down, your little one will toddle over with a book for you to read; even the child's naptime is not your own entirely, for as long as the child is in earshot (who knows if he is actually asleep?), he can hear and will imitate anything you say or do, including any improper word you use, any loss of temper at a broken garbage disposal—no, as a mother, your life is no longer your own.

But these changes are not burdensome to you; in fact, they occur quite naturally. Your very thoughts are no longer focused on yourself and your own comfort and well-being; all of a sudden, you become completely wrapped up in the comfort and joys of your little child. As much as you enjoy dressing up, suddenly you will care more about choosing your little girl's Sunday dress than about making sure you, yourself, have a new dress to wear. As much as you appreciate your succulent dessert, you cannot relax and eat if your little boy is having trouble chewing pieces of banana that were not cut up quite small enough.

But is this not the essence of Christianity? To think of others before ourselves, to love their comfort as our own and to serve them daily with joy and patience? Is this not how Christ Himself acted? And is not motherhood, thus, the perfect training camp for the Christian soul? Further, is not pregnancy the ideal way to prepare for this training? Does it not divorce from our hearts our love of comfort and our preoccupation with self? Does it not remind us constantly of the beauty and the value of suffering for others? Is it not a school of love, and thus our own unique path to Christ, who is Love Itself?

⊸ 36 ⊷

Post Partum

"A woman, when she is in labor, hath sorrow, because her
hour is come; but when she hath brought forth the child,
she remembereth no more the anguish, for joy that
a man is born into the world." (John 16:21).

GENERALLY, the period of time directly following childbirth is more joyous, but also more
difficult, than you expect it to be. First of all,
you are recovering from giving birth; secondly, you are
learning to care for your precious but very demanding
infant; thirdly, you need more sleep than ever and yet
you can scarcely find time to lie down; fourthly, you
are experiencing a drop in hormones, which causes a
corresponding plunge in your emotions; lastly, if you
are breastfeeding, you are trying to teach your baby
how to suck while growing accustomed yourself to this
rewarding, but initially uncomfortable, ritual. Other
problems, such as engorgement, hemorrhoids, recovery
from an episiotomy or a Caesarean section may afflict
you as well.

Further, many women experience "baby blues" the
week after giving birth, while others suffer from more
severe post partum depression for several more weeks.
Women who have had unplanned Caesarean sections
are especially vulnerable, both because their physical
recovery takes longer and because psychologically they
often feel that they have "failed" at giving birth. Baby
blues and post partum depression both make a challenging time even more trying.

The joys of motherhood are just beginning, but although pregnancy and childbirth are over, the sacrifices are not. At times, your exhilaration in cuddling your new baby knows no bounds. But this exhilaration is not enough to overcome the fatigue, the healing tissue, the sore nipples and the discouragement you feel at other times. No, once again, you must not look to earthly things to satisfy and encourage you. You must look higher. You must seek God. However difficult or trying this period may be, there is no aching or discouraged heart that does not benefit from turning to Our Lord in prayer.

Time is a precious commodity. When you feed your infant eight or nine times a day, every spare minute is taken up in catching up on sleep . . . or housework . . . or tending your other children, who do not understand why Mommy is too busy to play with them. Nevertheless, you cannot neglect your prayer life. This would be fatal, not only to your spiritual life, but even to your sanity, for only God can sustain you amid the difficulties you are encountering; only Our Lady can help you find joy and fulfillment in the rewards of your challenging vocation. If you have no other time to pray, converse with God as you sit and nurse your infant in the wee hours of the morning, when there is nothing to do but watch that tiny mouth suck . . . or perhaps read a book . . . or pray. You may not feel as pious or as inspired as you would if you sat down leisurely with some spiritual reading, but how often in the next few weeks will you find the time to do that? There will always be something else to do.

Pray, therefore, when you can, and lift your heart to Our Lord. Tell Him of your difficulties, of your needs; ask Him to give you the strength, the energy, and above all, the love to keep going. Thank Him for the gift of this precious baby, and ask Him that you may be worthy, for this baby is not only a gift, but a grave respon-

sibility as well. (The spiritual responsibility begins with
having the baby baptized as soon as possible. Then the
soul of this little one will be perfectly pure and innocent, free from Original Sin. Then you will have given
the greatest gift possible to your baby—the inheritance
of Heaven! Your baby will be a child of God, an heir
to Heaven, a member of the Mystical Body of Christ,
a temple of the Holy Spirit. Your child will be in the
state of Sanctifying Grace. If God should take him from
this earth now, his soul would go straight to Heaven.
Surely there is no excuse to delay baptizing your child
and bestowing on him such benefits of infinite value!)

Consequently, although you may not have time to
sit and meditate, you can at least offer your work each
day, your discomfort, your tiredness, to Our Lord. These
are gifts He will not despise. Also, develop the habit
of saying various aspirations—one-sentence prayers—
throughout the day; you can find a selection in most
Catholic prayerbooks, and you can memorize a few and
repeat them regularly throughout the day. Be sure to
have holy pictures in your house, and make an effort
to repeat an aspiration every time you pass by a particular picture. Be sure to hang a holy picture over the
sink, to remind yourself to offer up your time spent
preparing meals and washing dishes; hang another one
near your favorite spot to feed the baby, to remind
yourself to offer up your difficulties in nursing. When
the baby begins to eat less frequently, resume your
daily meditation as soon as you can; but in these early
weeks, your first priority is to fulfill your duties to
your family, and offer those to God. Your daily duty
done with a cheerful heart will please Him more than
anything else. This, in itself, is a prayer—your unique
prayer, that only you can offer to Him.

Also, as you nurse your little one, turn to the Blessed
Mother. Meditate on that first Christmas morning,
when she first nursed her newborn Baby. Think of how

joyfully she rose at the odd hours of the night to serve her King. Then remember that you too are serving your King in caring for your baby with a cheerful and loving heart. Consider that Mary would never complain to St. Joseph, but would only suggest what she or her Baby needed. How sweetly she greeted St. Joseph each morning, though perhaps she had slept little; how she thanked him for each small task he performed for her, until she could resume keeping house for them. Think of that difficult journey to Egypt, a trip made with haste and in secrecy, and with a small child in tow; think of Our Lady's maternal heart, aching at the sight of her loved ones driven into exile, but trusting always in the providential care of the Father. Complaints and anxieties were not for her. Only love. She loved God and trusted in His love. Rather than complain over hardships, she looked to see how her love could make things better for others. Love enabled her to bear the trials and woes of life, the little heartaches and difficulties, as well as the big ones. Love defined her vocation. Her vocation was to love.

And so is yours. It is love that will enable you to bear the discomfort of recovering from childbirth, perhaps from your episiotomy, or the much greater cross of recovering from a Caesarean section. It is love that will sustain you through the sleep deprivation that comes from arising every two or three hours to feed a crying baby. (Remember, sleep deprivation will affect your moods and emotions; accept the fact that you will be a little more emotional at times until your sleep schedule is a little more regular. Make sure your husband realizes the cause of your moodiness, too. It will help him to know *why* you are acting differently.) It is love that will ensure that you put off unnecessary tasks so that you can take your daily nap, even if it involves sacrifice, for your family will be far happier in a less-than-perfectly-clean house if you are at least somewhat well-rested and thus able to deal with every-day annoyances with calmness and peace. It is love that will impel you to breastfeed, despite the initial discomfort.* In time, you will find breastfeeding incredibly convenient, inexpensive and fulfilling—but it is not easy during those first few weeks, and you may not realize that it will get better. It *will*, slowly but surely. In the meantime, remember that, in losing sleep to feed your baby and by enduring the discomforts of breastfeeding, you continue to surrender your body out of love for your baby and for Our Lord. Do not give up. Pray especially to Our Lady for the grace to persevere in this intimate way of nourishing and nurturing your baby. This is a difficult, but very rewarding *labor of love.*

For those who suffer the misfortune of being unable to breastfeed their infants—for whatever reason—learn to accept the situation as God's holy will. Certainly there is no reason for feeling guilty over a situation beyond your control. It may be a blow to your pride, perhaps even to your self-esteem as a mother, that you cannot nurture your baby in this very special way. But trust that God knows what is best for you and your baby. You have surrendered yourself up to Him in pregnancy and childbirth; do the same now, in this difficulty. Know that, thanks to modern science, you can nourish your baby more than adequately with formula, and you can nurture your baby in a very intimate and fulfilling way by holding him and cuddling him throughout every feeding. Also, remember to have recourse to

---

*For expert, practical advice concerning any breastfeeding problems, call La Leche League, an international breastfeeding support group. Remember that while breastfeeding is uncomfortable at first, it should not be painful except for the initial latching-on. If you find it painful, even after the baby has latched on and is nursing, there is probably a problem that needs to be addressed. Calling a member of La Leche League may help you identify and correct the difficulty.

Venerable Zelie Martin, who herself was unable to nurse her children. Further, because there was no formula in her day, her babies had to live at the house of a wet-nurse, instead of at home. How this separation must have tried her maternal heart! But once again, she endured this trial with fortitude because she wanted what was best for her children—in short, because she loved them. Love does not seek self-satisfaction or approval from others, but only the good of the loved one. Love makes all sacrifices worthwhile.

A special word is in order for mothers who already have children and who are trying to juggle ministering to a newborn at all hours of the day and night with caring for all the needs of the older children, some of whom may not yet be old enough to understand why Mommy does not have as much time for them as she did before. During the first two months or so, when the baby is eating about eight times a day and is waking you up at all hours of the night, you must accept the fact that not everything in the household will run according to your usual standards. Baths might be given a day late; the cleaning may not get done; occasionally, sandwiches or a frozen dinner might have to suffice for the main meal; you will be tired and make stupid mistakes during the course of the day.

How difficult this time is may depend on how helpful your husband is. Nevertheless, whether he helps out or not, the household work may have to slide to some degree, and you must accept this, knowing that it is a temporary stage and will pass. If you allow your passion for order and your frustration over the reigning disorder to rule you, then this time will be absolutely miserable. Once again, you would be thinking in terms of *surviving*, instead of in terms of *living*. This is a difficult time, but it should also be a very special time, bonding with your newborn baby and allowing your other children to get to know their new sibling. Try to prioritize by making lists of things you have to do. Be sure to nap every day, and occasionally spend time with your older children, instead of doing unnecessary housework. All these things will help a lot.

But nothing will really help unless you realize that your vocation is not primarily to be a housekeeper, although that is part of it. No, primarily your vocation is to help your husband and your children to become as much like Christ as they possibly can. The best way to achieve this is by acting like Christ yourself—not by running your household perfectly, but by dealing with the imperfections in a Christ-like way—cheerfully, prayerfully, gently, lovingly. Reflect on this, and allow it to permeate your day. Remind yourself every morning, "My only job today is to love my husband and children as Christ loves them." Say this every morning. It will take a huge burden off of your shoulders. It will change your whole perspective on your vocation.

Post partum is a time of great joy and great exhaustion, waves of exhilaration and bursts of tears. But one glance at your baby is enough. To bring forth a new human life, to co-operate in the creation of a tiny, intricate body that is endowed by God with an immortal soul, to minister to the every need of one of God's little ones during the most impressionable and vulnerable years of his life — what other work could be more beautiful? What could be more noble? What other work could be more fulfilling than this, *your labor of love*?

Appendices

❧ Appendix I ❧

Miscarriage and Stillborn Delivery

"Behold a dead man was carried out, the only son of his mother; and she was a widow: and a great multitude of the city was with her. Whom when the Lord had seen, being moved with mercy towards her, he said to her: Weep not."
(Luke 7:12-13).

TRAGICALLY, some mothers lose their babies during pregnancy due to miscarriage, while others deliver stillborn babies. This is indeed a very difficult cross to bear, for you have rejoiced in your motherhood and suffered the discomforts of pregnancy, and now, it may seem, all for naught. If you have lost a child in either of these ways, be assured that your rejoicing and your suffering were not in vain, for you are still a mother, although your baby has parted from you. Your baby was created with an immortal soul, and because you gave him the gift of life, brief though it was, his soul still lives, and will continue to live forever. Because you accepted this new life from God, now and forever there is a soul in eternity who will give glory to God by his very existence, will never know pain or sorrow and who will never commit a sin. This human being will rejoice eternally that you were open to new life, that you conceived him, and that he lives forever in the merciful care of our loving God. You may want to choose a name for your departed baby, or even a Patron Saint to commend him to.

111

Naturally, a bereaved mother wants to know what happens to the soul of her departed little one after his death. In the rare instance that the child is still alive upon delivery—whether delivery takes place in the hospital, at home, or anywhere else—he should be baptized immediately.* Then you will know for certain that your baby knows the eternal joy of Heaven. You can pray to your baby, knowing he is now a saint and that he is watching over your family in a special way and waiting for you to join him in Heaven.

If there is even a *possibility* that the miscarried or stillborn child is still alive—no matter how tiny or undeveloped he may be, and even though he may not show any motion—he should be baptized *conditionally.**

The Church has never declared definitively what happens to the souls of unbaptized babies. However, there are several theories propounded by respected Catholic theologians on this issue. Some propose that unbaptized babies go to a place called Limbo, where they enjoy happiness and peace, although they do not experience the Beatific Vision of God that constitutes Heaven. Others suggest that the souls of unbaptized babies undergo some sort of test to determine their eternal destiny, involving some form of baptism of desire to make possible their entrance into Heaven—which is one reason why parents should pray for these children's souls. Still others hold that the desire of parents to baptize their babies might constitute a baptism of desire, in which case those babies would indeed know the eternal joy of Heaven.

In any case, you must *trust* in the goodness and mercy of God, who created your baby out of love and in whose tender care your dear baby rests. Whether

---

*See Appendix III, page 120, "Baptism in an Emergency." —*Publisher*, 2003.

or not your baby was baptized (many mothers do not even know this should be done), *put your baby in God's hands*. Your trust in God regarding a person so close to you will please Him *very much*. In the case of an unbaptized baby, your trust in God will count as a continual prayer for your departed baby.

Miscarriage and stillborn delivery are very, very painful, both physically and emotionally. You need time to rest and to grieve. Remember always that you are not alone in your grief. Turn to Our Lady of Sorrows. She, too, lost her Child—her only Son. She watched in untold agony as her Son suffered an excruciating death. She had not even her own dear husband with whom to share her burden, for he had already passed on.

Even after the joy of the Resurrection, Mary found herself alone again after the Ascension of Our Lord into Heaven. St. John, the Beloved Disciple, took her under his care, but it was not the same. The loneliness of her pure soul, whom no one on earth could fully understand, mystifies us now, as does her deep, unwavering trust in God, who filled her heart with calm and peace, even through those difficult years. Having known such great sorrow herself, she has comforted countless mothers who have lost their children at various ages.

How many of her daughters, upon drinking the dregs of bitterest grief, have found sympathy and strength in her Sorrowful Heart! Many of the Saints lost their children and found the courage to carry on only in the bosom of the Mother of Sorrows. For example, St. Dorothy of Montau lost eight of her nine children at tender ages; St. Hedwig lost three of her seven children during their childhood, and lived to see another three die in adulthood; Venerable Zelie Martin lost four of her nine children in childhood, some in infancy. Fortunately, many of Venerable Zelie's letters have been preserved, and the passages where she describes her devastation upon losing her little ones are particularly heartrending. It is clear that sanctity did not in any way make her motherly heart less human; but it is clear also that she found great comfort in remembering that these four baptized souls were safe and happy in Heaven, and she prayed to them frequently.* Certainly these saintly women, and others too numerous to name, found shelter from life's emotional storms in Mary's arms. And truly Mary's maternal heart aches with you in *your* pain and longs to console you. She who has suffered so deeply remains near you at all times, bolstering your bereaved heart and flooding your weary soul with grace.

Although during these difficult days you may require time by yourself, do not shut out your husband from your grief. He is grieving, too. Moreover, he hates to see you in pain and longs to ease your suffering. In these dark days, sharing your sufferings with your husband will lighten the burden for both of you, as well as strengthen the bond between you, helping you grow in mutual love and sympathy.

Even more, during this difficult time, do not shut out Christ. This will be a temptation, for is He not the Lord of life? Did He not take away your child, perhaps your only child, upon whom you would have lavished so much love? Usually, in such cases you cannot understand *why* these things happen. Probably, you never will—in this life. But nevertheless, you must trust in Our Lord, who knows all things and who loves you dearly. If you turn away from Him, you shut off your one Source of spiritual healing and hope. Rather, you should reflect often on His tender compassion for the widow of Naim, the body of whose only son was being carried out to be buried. He said to her, "Weep not."

---

* See *The Story of a Family: The Home of St. Thérèse of Lisieux*, by Fr. Stéphane-Joseph Piat, O.F.M., 1948, TAN reprint 1994.

He says the same to you. He sees your sorrow; He knows exactly what you are going through; He knows the depth of pain that you feel. He too has wept over death. Have you ever wondered why He shed tears over the death of Lazarus? After all, He knew He was going to raise him back to life. Why, then, did He weep? While no one can read the mind of Christ, we can speculate that perhaps He wept, not because His friend had died and was lost to Him, for He knew He would see him again soon, but because Lazarus and his sisters—and indeed the whole human race—had to endure death at all.

Perhaps He wept over the pain Lazarus and his sisters had suffered, and over the pain that the two sisters were still suffering. Perhaps He wept because, although Lazarus would be raised from the dead this time, he would still have to die again, at a later date, with no such joyous miracle to comfort his loved ones. Perhaps He wept over the suffering that all mankind must undergo in dying and watching loved ones die. Perhaps His mind flashed back to that sad day in His home in Nazareth when He held His foster father's rough hands for the last time and heard his gentle voice utter his final words. Perhaps His thoughts lept ahead in time to His own mother's desolation beneath the shadow of His cross. Perhaps He saw the pain of many mothers through the ages weeping over their own departed little ones—children often too little for them to know, but not too little for them to love. Perhaps He thought of you. Perhaps, then, it was not so much the death of Lazarus, but the fact of death itself that caused Him to weep. He who loved so deeply could not encounter the pain of His brethren without suffering acutely in the recesses of His own tender Heart.

And now He reaches out to you, yearning to press you to His Sacred Heart, to share your grief, to comfort you and give you hope. Do not push Him away.

Abandon yourself to Him with confidence. Say, although you may not feel it, "Lord, I trust in Thee." Repeat it, over and over, like the Jewish man who cried, "I do believe, Lord; help my unbelief." (*Mark* 9:23). Our Lord knows the effort it takes to say those few words during your time of sorrow, and He will in time reward you by allowing you once more to feel trust in your heart and to experience true peace and joy, knowing your precious baby will live forever in His merciful care. Truly, motherhood involves suffering. But it is not a useless suffering, for it is a suffering of love!

When you are able to, make a visit to the Blessed Sacrament. When you feel the Real Presence of the voluntary Prisoner of Love, locked inside the golden tabernacle because of His own compassion and yearning for souls, then you will not feel alone. True, you are experiencing great suffering. But He is not demanding anything of you that He Himself has not undergone first. Visit Him, lay your sufferings before Him in His voluntary little prison cell, and offer up to the Heavenly Father these sufferings of yours in union with Our Lord. This will undoubtedly be your most painful *labor of love*.

∽ Appendix II ∽

A Sample "Letter to the Editor" on Birth Control

"But sanctify the Lord Christ in your hearts, being ready always to satisfy every one that asketh you a reason of that hope which is in you." (1 Peter 3:15).

T HE Letters to the Editor section of any newspaper or magazine is one of the most popular features of each issue. Therefore, writing "letters to the editor" in order to support the truth and expose error is an invaluable apostolate in which almost anyone can participate. Many topics related to marriage and motherhood, besides that of birth control, can and should be addressed by Catholic readers. However, because we are dealing here primarily with the type of pregnancy and parenting magazines commonly given to expectant mothers at their doctors' offices (which can also usually be found on magazine racks in a drugstore), and since these magazines are particularly notorious for routinely promoting and advertising contraceptives, here we will discuss writing a letter on this particular topic.

Now, before you begin to write your letter to the editor, take a look at the letters to the editor in the issue to which you are objecting. Count how many words are in the average letter, and remember that editors tend to print short letters more often than long ones, and they also tend to edit longer ones. Furthermore, readers read the shorter letters first. Therefore, it is best to be as concise as possible.

Here is one sample letter that may help you get started. (The following letter contains 145 words.)

Editor, *(Name of Periodical)*,

I was saddened to see the ad for *(Brand Name of Birth Control)* in your *(date or month)* issue. Few people know that oral contraceptives *(or whatever type of contraceptive)* frequently fail to prevent conception and instead induce very early spontaneous abortion, without the mother's ever realizing she was pregnant. Further, contraception is a leading cause of divorce, for it changes the sacred act between spouses from an expression of unconditional love—a true donation of self and a true acceptance of the other—to an act of self-gratification. Until 1930, all Christian churches taught that contraception was morally wrong; they also recognized it to be harmful to marriage. Since contraception has been accepted by most Christian denominations, the divorce rate has sky-rocketed. As a young Catholic mother, I am proud to belong to that Faith which truly values the sanctity of marriage, and I am disturbed to see a family magazine sponsor such anti-family advertisements.

Your Full Name
Your Town and State

The above letter could be shortened or lengthened, according to the average length of letters in the periodical in question, and it could easily be adapted to be a response to an article on contraception rather than to an advertisement for a specific contraceptive.

Of course, there are many other points which you could bring up in such a letter, some of which you may find in other sections of this book. But do not try to mention them all; remember, you are submitting a letter, not an article! You cannot present all of the arguments necessary to convince all of the subscribers to stop practicing contraception immediately.

Your letter may not actually cause *anyone* to change his mind upon reading it. But changing the reader's mind instantaneously is not your purpose. What your letter should do is make the reader stop to think about the serious matter in question. It should bother him throughout the rest of his day. It may even pique his curiosity. If all you accomplish is to make someone aware that there may be some kind of reasoning behind the Church's teaching on birth control, which hitherto he had simply dismissed as an incomprehensibly outdated point of view, then you have succeeded. You have sown a seed. You have caused someone to doubt for just a moment his own secular attitudes. You have perhaps made someone just a little bit more open to the truth, so that when God chooses to touch that person's soul, in the near or distant future, He will find a little seed already planted there and ready for His grace to work.

❧ Appendix III ❧

Baptism in an Emergency

*"Can a woman forget her infant, so as not to have pity
on the son of her womb? And if she should forget,
yet will not I forget thee."* (Isaias 49:15).

IN a case of stillbirth or miscarriage, if there is any
possibility that the child is still alive—no matter
how tiny or undeveloped he may be—he should be
baptized.

Baptism is conferred by pouring ordinary water on
the head of the one to be baptized and pronouncing at
the same time the words:

"I baptize you in the name of the Father, and of the
Son, and of the Holy Ghost."

The baby or fetus, no matter at what stage of pregnancy, should be baptized unconditionally (that is, using
the above formula) if certainly alive; if life is doubt-
ful, the child should be baptized *conditionally*. Any
motion on the part of the premature fetus may be
taken as a sign of certain life. Lack of motion, however, is not a sure sign of death.

The formula for *conditional* Baptism is: "If you can
be baptized, I baptize you in the name of the Father,
and of the Son, and of the Holy Ghost."

If, when delivered, the fetus is enclosed in membranes, *these membranes should always be opened
completely* so that Baptism may be conferred directly
on the head itself of the premature child, not on the
membranes.

For a fetus or embryo delivered in the early stages of pregnancy, Baptism by immersion is a surer and better method. The manner of Baptism by immersion is as follows: When the membrane has been broken, the fetus is completely immersed in water and withdrawn *while* the person who is baptizing pronounces the words of Baptism.

If immersion in such cases is not immediately possible, rather than permit a dangerous delay, the water may be poured directly over the fetus that has been exposed by the opening of the membranes.

Mothers should be very well instructed in this matter of Baptism. In the case of a miscarriage or in any danger of death for an unbaptized child, they should either endeavor to have the Baptism performed by others or should perform it themselves.

Those who attend a pregnant woman in the time of an actual or imminent miscarriage should be on the alert to rescue the fetus and to perform the necessary Baptism. At least *conditional* Baptism should be given, even though there is no direct evidence of life whatever.

In an emergency, if a Catholic is not available, Baptism may be administered by anyone, whether or not he or she is Catholic, or even Christian (and even if the person baptizing does not believe in Baptism, as long as he or she intends—in a general way at least—to do what the Church does by baptizing).

Baptism removes the "stain" of Original Sin from the child's soul and gives him Sanctifying Grace, a sharing in the life of God Himself. Thus he becomes a child of God and an heir of Heaven. A baby or fetus who dies after Baptism goes directly to Heaven and will be a saint of God for all eternity.

(This Appendix adapted by the Publisher from *Mothers' Manual: Helps for Mothers and Expectant Mothers*, by Rev. A. Francis Coomes, S.J., Imprimatur ✚ John J. Carberry, 1970. Hirten Co., Brooklyn, 1984.)

Prayers for Mothers

"Always rejoice. Pray without ceasing. In all things give thanks; for this is the will of God in Christ Jesus concerning you all." (1 Thessalonians 5:17-18).

Prayer of an Expectant Mother to Jesus, The Lord of Life

"What shall I render to the Lord, for all the things that he hath rendered to me?" (Psalms 115:12).

DEAR Jesus, Lord of life, how can I express my gratitude to Thee for the precious new life growing within me? How can I thank Thee for the glorious and miraculous privilege of motherhood? In awe do I realize that there is a new human being growing in my womb. In wonder I recognize that Thou hast entrusted an innocent soul into my care! In fear do I remember that I am responsible for the formation—spiritual and physical—of this child. And in supplication I beg for Thy merciful assistance.

O Jesus, help me in my pregnancy to prepare for the awesome vocation of motherhood. May I not grumble through morning sickness and other discomforts, but use each trial as a means of growing closer to Thee and to prepare myself to be a patient, wise and loving mother. It is hard, in my human nature, for me to see any good in suffering, Dear Jesus. But it is enough to know that Thou, quite freely, didst choose to suffer. Thou hast blessed and sanctified suffering, in all its varieties—spiritual, emotional and physical. Thou hast given me a reason for hope. If Thou hast suffered unfathomable agonies for me, then I, with Thy grace, can suffer my little discomforts and inconveniences for Thee. And perhaps Thou, in Thine infinite mercy, will see my little offering and bless me with the grace to be a good and holy mother.

For I so desperately need this grace. Left to myself, I am selfish, inconsiderate, impatient, proud, imprudent, lazy, greedy, neglectful of prayers and complaining about duties. Only with Thy grace may I grow to be the patient, wise, prayerful and loving mother I long to be and that my baby needs. O Lord, help me to neglect Thy grace no longer, but to make the effort to pray to Thee frequently, to meditate on Thy Word daily, to think of Thee as I work, to follow Thine inspirations faithfully, to fulfill my duties willingly and even cheerfully.

Dear Jesus, protect my baby and me from all harm, physical and spiritual. May I face childbirth with peace and courage, and may my childbirth go smoothly, without any complications. Grant that my baby will receive the blessed gift of Baptism, and live his life in grace and in truth.

O Lord, I do not know how to thank Thee for the beautiful gift of life that Thou hast given me! Make me worthy of Thy gift; teach me to imitate Thine own sinless Mother in my efforts to raise my child to be healthy, happy and holy. Amen.

Prayer to Our Lady,
Model and Mother of Mothers

"And Mary said: Behold the handmaid of the Lord; be it done to me according to thy word." (Luke 1:38).

D EAR Mary, Model and Mother of mothers, please be with me throughout this pregnancy, and indeed, throughout my life.

◇ Be with me when I feel sick, tired or irritable. Obtain for me the strength to speak and act cheerfully and charitably, and to offer my sufferings up to your Son with love and joy. May I see all my discomforts, inconveniences and annoyances as opportunities to grow closer to Him and to repay Him in a small way for all that He has done for me. During my most hectic or difficult days, remind me to take a moment to pray for grace and strength, and then return to my work singing a hymn to thee.

◇ Be with me, Blessed Mother, as I work. May I handle each task and each situation with the serenity which characterized thine own work in thy home in Nazareth. May I make my home a haven for my husband and children, filled with the peace and joy that comes from loving and trusting in God.

◇ Be with me, Blessed Mother, as I go to the doctor's each month. Strengthen me as I go through all the necessary tests and procedures, that once again, I may view all as opportunities to suffer for Christ. Keep up my courage, and protect the health and well-being of my little baby and myself, for thou art the mother of both of us.

◇ Be with me, Blessed Mother, as I go into labor, and assist me through childbirth. Help me not to fear the pain, but to embrace it. May I not lose sight of the reason why I am suffering—for the sake of my beautiful little baby—and even more, for love of thy Divine Son, Jesus. During these difficult moments, protect my baby and me from all harm. Obtain that my childbirth goes smoothly, quickly and without any complications.

◇ Be with me, Blessed Mother, as I breastfeed my child. Help my baby to learn quickly the art of sucking, and protect me from the various difficulties that sometimes accompany breastfeeding. Encourage me during the initial discomfort, and surround me with knowledgeable nurses who can best advise and assist me in any difficulties. Help me to nourish my baby in this uniquely fulfilling and nurturing way.

◇ Be with me, Blessed Mother, throughout all my life. Show me how to be a mother. Show me how to love and nurture the innocent soul entrusted to my care; show me how and when to encourage, to discipline, to teach and to form my child to be a holy, healthy and happy Christian. Help me to be patient, calm, consistent, prayerful, wise and loving. No matter how busy I am, may Christ always be the Center of my life, as He always was of thine.

Blessed Virgin Mary, help me always to be, like thee, a good Christian wife and mother! Amen.

Prayer to St. Joseph, Protector of Families

"Joseph her husband, being a just man . . ." (Matthew 1:19).

D EAR St. Joseph, Protector of families, please pray for my family.

◇ Pray for my husband. Help him to be a good Christian husband and father. Help him to find satisfaction and fulfillment in his work, which is so necessary to the support of our family. Help him to be truly the head of our family—to lead the family in prayer, in virtue, in work and in play. May he always have time to spend with our family, giving the children a good example of a Christian man and providing them with the fatherly love and attention they need, as well as giving me the support and love I need as his wife.

◇ Pray also for (my children, especially) the baby growing within me. Keep in good health all the children I have or will ever have; but more than this, keep them close to thy Foster Child, Jesus Christ. May they learn to love Him and to serve God throughout their lives, and may they never be separated from Jesus, Our Lord.

◇ Lastly, good St. Joseph, please pray for me. Help me to be a good mother to my children. I am weak, proud and selfish. Often I allow my discomforts or mood swings to make me irritable. Help me to overcome my weaknesses, to be a kind and patient mother and a loving and understanding wife. Help me to prepare for the birth of my baby, not with anxiety and bustle, but with prayer. May I learn from my pregnancy to face all trials with peace and love. Help me to trust God, as thou didst, in all the events of my life, from childbirth, to raising my children and until my last breath.

St. Joseph, Protector of Families and Patron of the Dying, help my family to live and die always united in Christ. Amen.

Prayer to an Unborn Baby's Guardian Angel

"See that you despise not one of these little ones: for I say to you, that their angels in heaven always see the face of my Father who is in heaven." (Matthew 18:10).

DEAR Guardian Angel, who has been appointed to watch over the child now sheltered in my womb, please guard and protect my baby, both now and throughout my baby's whole life. Keep my baby in good health. Obtain that my baby will survive childbirth and have the priceless privilege of receiving the Sacrament of Baptism, thus becoming a child of God and an heir to Heaven. May my child learn to love God and His Church, and may my child's innocent soul never be tainted by mortal sin. Keep my child faithful to the promises we will make for him at his Baptism, and help him to frequent the Sacraments of Confession and Communion throughout his life. May he grow healthy and strong, and may he, as an adult, find himself happy, healthy and unwavering in his Catholic faith. And finally, may I meet my child once again in Heaven.

Dear Guardian Angel, help me, as the mother of this child, to guide him lovingly and wisely. Help me to understand his physical, emotional and spiritual needs, and to fill them as only a mother can. Pray both for my baby and for me, that I may cooperate with God's grace and help my child as best I can along the path to Heaven. Amen.

Prayer to St. Gerard,
Patron of Expectant Mothers

"Pray for one another, that you may be saved.
For the continual prayer of a just man availeth much."
(James 5:16).

O ST. GERARD, assist me in my pregnancy. Protect the physical health of my child and myself throughout pregnancy and childbirth. Even more, protect the spiritual health of my child and myself. Help me to endure my sufferings with patience, love and peace, and obtain that my child's soul may receive the Sacrament of Baptism and thus become a child of God. Intercede for me that I may bear the pains of childbirth with grace and courage, and that my childbirth may go smoothly and quickly, with no medical problems for my baby or myself. Above all, pray that my child and I may live holy lives and may meet once again in the eternal joy of Heaven. Amen.

St. Gerard, pray for us!

St. Anne, pray for us!

NOTE: Although it may seem odd that a man was chosen to be the Patron Saint of expectant mothers, expectant mothers have traditionally invoked St. Gerard because, on more than one occasion during his life, he miraculously helped women who were having difficulty in labor. Therefore, let us, too, ask his intercession for help in our own pregnancies and labors!

Prayer of an Expectant Mother on Bedrest

"Rejoicing in hope. Patient in tribulation. Instant in prayer."
(Romans 12:12).

O LORD, the days pass so slowly in anxious waiting! At times I feel so worried about my unborn baby; at other times, I just feel restless and frustrated because there is so much to be done, and I am not allowed to do anything but lie here and wait. Help me to be patient, remembering always that for the time being, I can serve Thee best, not by action, but by inaction—by cheerful obedience to my doctor, thereby protecting the health of my child, and by offering my boredom and discomfort to Thee. I remember in particular the souls in Purgatory, who are also waiting helplessly, but hopefully, for their great day of deliverance, and I offer some of my suffering for them.

During this time of bedrest, may I not become angry or discouraged, but rather grow closer to Thee. May I use the extra time I have to pray and meditate, thus preparing myself for the joys, challenges and responsibilities of motherhood. How could I better prepare myself for anything than by spending extra time with Thee? And what a beautiful way to prepare and renew my spirit for this wonderful vocation!

But to maintain a peaceful, positive attitude which views bedrest as an opportunity to grow in love, I need Thy grace. Grant patience and strength to me, to my family, and to all those who are caring for me or helping me run my household. Lastly, merciful Jesus, protect and bless the precious baby in my womb. May my baby be born strong and healthy at the proper time, and may my baby receive the precious gift of the Sacrament of Baptism. Amen.

Prayer During a Crisis Pregnancy

"Let not your heart be troubled. You believe in God, believe also in me." (John 14:1).

(Women in "unplanned" pregnancies, whether they have been using birth control to avoid conception or whether they conceived outside of marriage, often face innumerable difficulties. However, Our Lord does not abandon them in their troubles, but seeks to unite them more closely to Himself by teaching them to trust in Him, though it may seem that all the world is against them. He says to them, "But have confidence, I have overcome the world." *John* 16:33).

DEAREST Jesus, I offer all my pain and anxieties to Thee. Thou knowest my situation, as well as the confusion and anguish that torment my heart. Thou hast sent me the gift of a new life, a new human being, growing here within my womb. How my heart would love to rejoice at this most wondrous gift! But my heart cannot rejoice. This new life, even now growing within me, has come at a time when I do not yet feel ready for the responsibility of motherhood. How can I take care of this child, O Lord? What will I do? My heart is heavy with worry, fear and gnawing guilt.

And yet I know, O Jesus, that "the foolishness of God is wiser than men" and that "the weak things of the world hath God chosen, that he may confound the strong." (*1 Corinthians* 1:25,27). Thy ways are not men's ways, and Thy wisdom is beyond men's understanding. So, although I cannot understand why Thou hast sent me a child at this time, O Lord, when I feel so helpless and unable to care for a baby, I believe that Thou hast done so out of Thine infinite goodness and love. I know that if I trust in Thee, Thou wilt not forsake me. As hopeless as my situation looks right now, as lonely and as lost as I feel right now, I trust that Thou art with me. I know that Thou wilt help me care for myself and my baby if I trust in Thee and place myself completely in Thy hands. Help me to do Thy will in all things, O Lord. I beg Thy forgiveness for all my past sins and ask that Thou wilt help me never to offend Thee again. I know that Thou wilt not hold my past sins against me, but that Thou only rejoicest that I have, in my troubles, turned to Thee. Grant that I may never forsake Thee, and that my love and trust in Thee will only grow each day. Calm my fears, Dear Jesus, strengthen my faith, and help me to make the best decisions possible for my baby and myself. Be with me at every moment. Guard and protect my baby and me in all our needs.

I feel so weak, O Lord, but I know that I do not need to be strong, for Thou wilt give me Thy strength. Assist me, O Lord, in the challenges that lie ahead; help me to trust in Thee, to take good care of myself and my baby, and to imitate Thine own Blessed Mother in my new vocation.

My Jesus, I give thee all my sufferings and all my troubles. Have mercy on me! Amen.

Prayer of a Bereaved Mother
of an Unbaptized Baby

"Blessed are they that mourn; for they shall be comforted."
(Matthew 5:5).

O MERCIFUL Jesus, hear me! Please listen to my plea for help. My heart is stricken, and my soul is overwhelmed with grief. I try to understand, but I can only trust. My God, I believe in Thee! Increase my faith. Strengthen my trust, for I feel so weak. Console my heart, for I know no comfort, now that I have lost my precious baby, whom Thou hadst given me. I do not know why Thou hast taken my child from me, but I know I must trust in Thy mercy and goodness. I know that Thou dost not delight in my sorrows, but dost love me with an infinite love and dost feel infinite compassion for my poor heart. Have mercy on me, Sweet Heart of Jesus, have pity on me in my grief, and comfort me. I know my little one is safe in Thy tender care. Have mercy on my baby, O Lord, and bless my baby and our grieving family.

O Sorrowful Heart of Mary, join me in my sorrow. Thou hast known the anguish of watching thy Son die; I too have lost my child. In my grief, I turn to thee, my Mother. Cover me with thy mantle, shower me with graces, and comfort me by thy presence. Assist me and my husband through this trying time; may our hearts draw even closer to each other and to Our Merciful Lord in this painful time. Help us to trust in His goodness and love, as thou didst trust, long ago, beneath the Cross of Calvary. As for our dear baby who has departed from us, I entrust this child to thy care. My child did not have the opportunity to receive the Sacrament of Baptism; nevertheless, take him under thy mantle, watch over him and pray for him. I know thy prayers have never failed before the Heavenly Throne.

And, O merciful Mother, watch over our family, comfort us in our grief, and help us to find peace and solace in trusting in the goodness and love of our merciful God, in whose care our dear baby rests. Amen.

Mother of Sorrows, pray for me!

Mother of Sorrows, pray for my husband!

Mother of Sorrows, pray for my departed child!

Prayer of a Bereaved Mother
of a Baptized Baby

"Jesus said to her: I am the resurrection and the life: he that believeth in me, although he be dead, shall live: And every one that liveth, and believeth in me, shall not die for ever."
(John 11:25-26).

O TENDER Heart of Jesus, please have mercy on my grieving heart! I have lost my child, and my soul is flooded with tears. And yet I know that Thou hast not abandoned me. Thou art with me always. Thou hast triumphed over death, so that through Sanctifying Grace, death is not the end of life, but only the beginning of a life of eternal joy and peace. Help me, O Lord, in this time of sorrow, to find consolation in knowing my child is now a saint and enjoys the perfect happiness of living with Thee in Heaven.

O Mary, my Sorrowful Mother, who gazed in sorrow at the sight of thy Son dying on the Cross, please pray for me and for my husband in our time of grief. Help us to find peace and comfort in trusting in our merciful Father's love. May this trial serve to strengthen the bond between our sorrowing hearts, to unite us even more closely to each other, and to deepen our faith and trust in God our Father. Though our sweet child is lost to us in this life, may we both know the unutterable joy of meeting our child again in Heaven.

Venerable Zelie Martin, mother of St. Therese the Little Flower, you experienced profound grief when you held four of your children in your arms as they breathed their last breath. Assist me in my grief, for I too have lost a child. You knew deep sorrow, yet you never grew bitter or angry against God, but always trusted in His infinite mercy and love. Help me to trust Him too. Your faith assured you that your little ones were happy in Heaven, and you found consolation in knowing they were watching over your family and praying for you. Help me, too, to be strengthened by my Catholic Faith, and to find joy in knowing that my precious child is now enjoying the peace and joy of Heaven.

All ye heavenly Angels and Saints, pray for us! Pray for our grieving family! May we never forget to pray to the little member of our family who is watching over us from Heaven. Amen.

Prayer During Post Partum Depression

"And going a little further, he fell upon his face, praying, and saying: My Father, if it be possible, let this chalice pass from me. Nevertheless, not as I will, but as thou wilt."
(Matthew 26:39).

DEAREST Lord Jesus, I feel I should be happy now that my baby is born at last, but alas, sorrow floods my heart. I do not know where to turn. Who can understand this sadness which I myself do not understand? But, O Lord, I know that Thou knowest my anguish. Thou alone dost understand the sorrow I feel. Thou dost understand it because Thou hast known such anguish too. But Thou didst accept Thy sorrow with the words, "Not as I will, but as Thou wilt." So I too pray to the Heavenly Father with Thee, my Jesus: "Not as I will, but as Thou wilt." Help me through this difficult time, O Lord. Grant me Thy strength, for I have none left. I beg Thee, O Jesus, to shorten my sufferings, if it be God's will; and in the meantime, be with me at every moment, nourish my poor soul with Thy grace, and send Thy sweet Mother, Our Lady of Consolation, to comfort me until my chalice of sorrow has passed.

Compassionate Jesus, I offer all my troubles to Thee; help me to bear them with courage and peace. Help me to be a good mother to my new baby, despite my trials. May my child(ren) and my husband not suffer from the difficulties I am experiencing. Watch over our family, O Lord, and grant that soon I may find joy and peace in caring for this precious child whom Thou hast sent to me in Thy love.

Tender Heart of Jesus, have mercy on me! Amen.

Prayer after Childbirth

"And Adam knew Eve his wife: who conceived and brought forth Cain, saying:
I have gotten a man through God." (Genesis 4:1).

O GOD, how can I thank Thee for the gift of this beautiful child? How perfect are his tiny hands and feet! How marvelous is his perfectly formed body! And how much more wonderful is the immortal soul which Thou hast created to inhabit this body, to brighten this world, and to praise Thee for all eternity in the next! What rich potential lies behind that infant face, so peaceful in repose, so expressive in distress, so unaware as yet of the marvels of Thy goodness!

Deign to make me worthy of this precious gift, this unutterable privilege, this wonderful responsibility which Thou hast seen fit to bestow upon me. With Thy holy Mother as my model, may I raise this child in truth and goodness, in virtue and in love. May I make my home a haven of peace and sanctity, safe from the corruption of the world—a home inspiring all who enter it to live nobler lives and assisting all who dwell here to keep their minds fixed on Thee. May this dear child be privileged to receive the Sacrament of Baptism very soon, and may my new little baby (and all my children) grow in the Faith, live a virtuous life, receive the Sacraments frequently and die in Thy grace.

Dear Jesus, how can I realize that Thou didst come

as a babe no bigger than the one I hold in my arms, who cannot even hold up his head or eat without assistance? What humility Thou hast taught us! What sacrifice! What love! In all the trials that lie before me as a mother, help me to imitate Thy selflessness and love, offering all my sufferings gladly to Thee, Who hast shown me how to suffer for love. May I trust in Thee through all difficulties, knowing that Thou hast foreseen them all and hast permitted them for my greater sanctification. May every joy and every trial be for me a step toward greater holiness, greater trust and greater love, for love is the vocation Thou hast given to me. Amen.

If you have enjoyed this book, consider making your next selection from among the following . . .

Prices subject to change.

St. Margaret Clitherow—"The Pearl of York." *Monro* 6.00
St. Vincent Ferrer. *Fr. Pradel, O.P.* 9.00
The Life of Father De Smet. *Fr. Laveille, S.J.* 18.00
Glories of Divine Grace. *Fr. Matthias Scheeben* 18.00
Holy Eucharist—Our All. *Fr. Lukas Etlin* 3.00
Hail Holy Queen (from *Glories of Mary*). *St. Alphonsus* 9.00
Novena of Holy Communions. *Lovasik* 2.50
Brief Catechism for Adults. *Cogan* 12.50
The Cath. Religion—Illus./Expl. for Child, Adult, Convert. *Burbach* . . . 12.50
Eucharistic Miracles. *Joan Carroll Cruz* 16.50
The Incorruptibles. *Joan Carroll Cruz* 16.50
Secular Saints: 250 Lay Men, Women & Children. PB. *Cruz.* 35.00
Pope St. Pius X. *F. A. Forbes* 11.00
St. Alphonsus Liguori. *Frs. Miller and Aubin* 18.00
Self-Abandonment to Divine Providence. *Fr. de Caussade, S.J.* 22.50
The Song of Songs—A Mystical Exposition. *Fr. Arintero, O.P.* 21.50
Prophecy for Today. *Edward Connor* 7.50
Saint Michael and the Angels. *Approved Sources* 9.00
Dolorous Passion of Our Lord. *Anne C. Emmerich* 18.00
Modern Saints—Their Lives & Faces, Book I. *Ann Ball* 21.00
Modern Saints—Their Lives & Faces, Book II. *Ann Ball.* 23.00
Our Lady of Fatima's Peace Plan from Heaven. *Booklet* 1.00
Divine Favors Granted to St. Joseph. *Père Binet* 7.50
St. Joseph Cafasso—Priest of the Gallows. *St. John Bosco.* 6.00
Catechism of the Council of Trent. *McHugh/Callan* 27.50
The Foot of the Cross. *Fr. Faber.* 18.00
The Rosary in Action. *John Johnson* 12.00
Padre Pio—The Stigmatist. *Fr. Charles Carty* 16.50
Why Squander Illness? *Frs. Rumble & Carty.* 4.00
Fatima—The Great Sign. *Francis Johnston* 12.00
Heliotropium—Conformity of Human Will to Divine. *Drexelius* 15.00
Charity for the Suffering Souls. *Fr. John Nageleisen.* 18.00
Devotion to the Sacred Heart of Jesus. *Verheylezoon.* 16.50
Who Is Padre Pio? *Radio Replies Press* 3.00
The Stigmata and Modern Science. *Fr. Charles Carty* 2.50
St. Anthony—The Wonder Worker of Padua. *Stoddard* 7.00
The Precious Blood. *Fr. Faber* 16.50
The Holy Shroud & Four Visions. *Fr. O'Connell* 3.50
Clean Love in Courtship. *Fr. Lawrence Lovasik.* 4.50
The Secret of the Rosary. *St. Louis De Montfort* 5.00
The History of Antichrist. *Rev. P. Huchede* 4.00
Where We Got the Bible. *Fr. Henry Graham.* 8.00
Hidden Treasure—Holy Mass. *St. Leonard* 7.50
Imitation of the Sacred Heart of Jesus. *Fr. Arnoudt* 18.50
The Life & Glories of St. Joseph. *Edward Thompson* 16.50
Humility of Heart. *Fr. Cajetan da Bergamo.* 9.00
The Curé D'Ars. *Abbé Francis Trochu* 24.00
Love, Peace and Joy. (St. Gertrude). *Prévot* 8.00
This Is The Faith. *Canon Francis Ripley.* 21.00

About the Author

Agnes M. Penny was born and raised in Norwood, Massachusetts, the youngest of twelve children. She graduated from Christendom College in Front Royal, Virginia in 1997, with a degree in English literature. She and her husband Daniel, who teaches theology at Allentown Central Catholic High School, were married in 1998. They currently reside in Whitehall, Pennsylvania with their three little girls, aged $3\frac{1}{2}$ years, $2\frac{1}{2}$ years, and 1 year old. The couple are currently expecting their fourth child.